The Path to Nibbāna

How Mindfulness of Loving-Kindness Progresses through the Tranquil Aware Jhānas to Awakening

By

David C. Johnson

ISBN-13: 978-1508808916
ISBN-10: 1508808910
BTS Publishing

Other Books by David Johnson

*A Guide to Tranquil Wisdom Insight Meditation,
 (A companion to this book)
BTS Publishing, Annapolis 2015

*Co-written with Bhante Vimalaraṁsi

"THE HOLY LIFE, friend Visākha, is grounded upon Nibbāna, culminates in Nibbāna, ends in Nibbāna."

Majjhima Nikāya 44, Cūḷavedalla Sutta

CONTENTS

Acknowledgments

I want to acknowledge Venerable Bhante Vimalaraṁsi Mahāthera, from whom I have learned this practice. He is the "founder" of Tranquil Wisdom Insight Meditation (TWIM). Without his skillful guidance, this project would not be possible. Descriptions for many of the jhānas have come from evening talks on the Anupada Sutta (MN 111) by Venerable Vimalaraṁsi. It was his struggle through years of intense meditation practice, and his discussions with many of the world's most venerable monks, that led him in an entirely different direction. He went back to the earliest Buddhist teachings, the suttas in the Pāli Canon, to practice what the Buddha himself had taught his own disciples. From this, he discovered TWIM and has given us this gift of true Dhamma.

I wish to thank the Venerable for reviewing this work and correcting misunderstandings which may have occurred.

I also acknowledge Bhikkhu Bodhi for his work The Middle Length Discourses of the Buddha: A Translation of the Majjhima Nikāya (Wisdom Publications: Somerville, MA, 1995) by Bhikkhu Bodhi and Bhikkhu Nāṇamoli — this book, with some exceptions, is the basis for TWIM meditation practice.

Thanks also to Brenda Ie-Mcrae, who wrote down a one-page summary, based on student interviews, of what meditators experienced as they progressed through the meditation process. Seeing the need to document the levels of practice, I expanded her summary to the book you now are reading.

Also, thanks to Teri Pohl, Paul Johnson, Mark and Antra Berger, Doug Kraft and J. Delmar who helped with editing and for their many useful suggestions. Thanks to S. Jordan who rendered the beautiful cover art from his own unique design.

Introduction.

The purpose of this book is to help the earnest seeker and advanced meditator understand the experiences and signposts on the Buddha's path, which has as its goal the destruction of craving and the elimination of ignorance. I want to document these experiences for the meditation community so they may be studied and preserved as a guide to future meditators.

This book was also written so that meditators without access to local teachers could have all the instructions to continue down this path on their own. Every instruction on how to meditate at every level is here. There are no secret techniques held back, just the words from the suttas and commentary by Venerable Bhante Vimalaraṁsi.

I have added to the edition you are now reading a review of all the instructions and all the progress steps and signposts in the last chapter of the book. So if you forget some of the steps, go there for a refresher and, perhaps, a higher level overview of all the meditation instructions in the book.

In this book are integrated all the instructions for the beginning meditator. If you are familiar with the starting instructions you can skip ahead to the section on the advanced chapters on Jhāna states. But, it's probably best to read the whole book, as you never know what you might pick up.

If, when you are starting, you bog down and you just can't feel this loving-kindness for yourself, take a look at the pamphlet, provided at the end of this book, by Bhante Vimalaramsi entitled, "A Guide to Forgiveness Meditation." Try this meditation and see if it doesn't loosen possible emotional blocks from past traumas, bosses or other scary memories! Forgiveness can be a perfect prerequisite to experiencing warm, flowing loving-kindness.

At some places in the book, I will put **"—Meditation Instruction:"** to highlight for students, who are using this book as an instruction guide, progressive directions on how to proceed with the practice.

TWIM is a fancy name for, basically, the Brahmavihāra practice, starting with mettā or loving-kindness as the object (breath may be used but tends to have slower progress). These instructions are taken directly from the meditation methods described in the suttas, the earliest Buddhist teachings. TWIM is the practice that will lead us to Nibbāna as it is outlined in the texts. We will see that when the instructions are followed, there are immediate results precisely as the Buddha laid out.

The Path to Nibbāna elaborates on both the goal and the practice of meditation as explained by the Buddha. Its purpose is to follow the progress of the practice as it is explained in the suttas themselves. For that, the clearest map is the Majjhima Nikāya (MN) No. 111, the Anupada Sutta, "One by One as they Occurred." This sutta shows how progress occurs step-by-step all the way to Nibbāna. This is the "map" we will use as we go through the levels of insight in this book.

The suttas of the Pāli Canon are traceable back 2,550 years to the Buddha himself. They are considered by scholars to be the words of the Buddha as he originally spoke them.

To put a finer point on this, it is thought that the Buddha spoke Magadhi. That was his native language. Pāli is a form of that language, and later, all of the suttas were documented in Pāli, first by reciting and then writing them down by members of the Buddhist Order in Sri Lanka.

They were written on palm leaves about 80 B.C.[i] As they were written down, monks, who had memorized the suttas, checked the written texts for any added or wrong words.

Introduction

The suttas were inscribed on stone tablets in Mandalay, Burma and are today still being memorized and recited by Buddhist monks in Burmese monasteries. This has continued since the first council of five hundred Senior Monks or *Arahants* convened three months after the Buddha died. I visited this interesting site in Burma in 2003 and saw the white marble stones with these very inscriptions.

Groups of monks memorize the sutta texts together. One monk will recite, and the rest of the group will check and correct him as he goes. This method has been about as foolproof as any other to retain original texts for long periods. Writing the suttas down can be subject to the translator's misinterpretation of what words to use, to describe the practice precisely.

But, even with this method, there could have been errors that crept in, even as perfect as this system was. We can't really know because we weren't there and it *was* over twenty-five centuries ago!

Thus, we use these suttas as the closest direct guide to what the Buddha really taught.

There are many Buddhist sects and many different beliefs and practices; all we can do is find what meditation practice matches the Buddha's words. The practice of TWIM is "new" in the sense it has been *rediscovered* in the suttas. It is not practiced very widely (yet), which seems rather surprising. In fact, Venerable Bhante Vimalaraṁsi and his approved teachers, are the only ones who teach directly from the suttas in this way. Others reference the suttas but don't follow them precisely. TWIM is the actual and correct application of Right Effort. This is the reason for its resulting success. I will discuss more about this later.

Changes have been made in other practices to allegedly "improve" upon the Buddha's meditation instructions. But, hold on, he was the Buddha! Is it not just a little bit presumptuous to think that the instructions of a Buddha can be improved upon? After all, he was indeed the supremely awakened Tathāgata, perfecting his wisdom over countless lifetimes.

Let's try to put aside all the other techniques for now and just focus on how to practice, as described in the early teachings, as close to the actual words of the Buddha as we can get. Most scholars agree that the Pāli Canon and its suttas are the actual teachings of the Buddha. So, let's go to them, and only them, to find the way to practice.

The Anupada Sutta, MN 111, explains the progress of the meditation through the jhānas and the *Four Foundations of Mindfulness* at the same time. It will be shown here that these jhānas when practiced *as taught in the suttas,* will lead us to awakening. The jhānas described in the Anupada Sutta are not to be confused with the concentration states commonly taught elsewhere. These are the *Tranquil Aware Jhānas* that are being taught in the suttas, in which you maintain awareness of both mind *and body*. Their foundation is *collectedness,* not concentration which we will cover later.

It is this rediscovered "aware jhāna" that is the key to a new understanding of the Buddha's teachings.

The TWIM technique referenced in this book uses for its primary sutta guide, *The Middle Length Discourses of the Buddha: A Translation of the Majjhima Nikāya,* by Bhikkhu Bodhi and Bhikkhu *Nāṇamoli.* Bhante Vimalaraṁsi feels this is the closest translation available, though sometimes he prefers different wordings then are used there. For example, he uses the word "habitual tendency" instead of "becoming." More on this later.

We will combine here the explanation of the suttas' meaning with the actual experiences of the many meditators who have practiced and have been successful. Also, we will attempt to explain some of the reasons why certain experiences and subtle phenomena occur — though, only the Buddha knows for sure. Please forgive me for errors and omissions.

Some phenomena like the subtlest links of dependent origination that are deep down in the mental processes have had their descriptions left out. They are for the student to discover on their own and it won't change the pace of a student's progress by not describing them here. Explaining certain phenomena before the student is ready to see them can create false expectations and wrong ideas.

Many students, later, are grateful that Bhante does not explain to them where they are in the jhānas. They just want to progress and not be thinking and analyzing as they practice. They may develop some sense of pride because of thoughts about "I am in this jhāna or that jhāna." They might have some familiarity with meditation practice and may have some conceit arise and get stuck thinking about how far advanced they are — when they are only beginners in this practice. It is better off not knowing where you are if you are on an intensive retreat and just follow the instructions.

If you are seeking an even deeper understanding of how the practice works than what is described here in this book, more descriptions of insights and levels of understanding that arise, and the sutta references that support this meditation, you may also want to read one of the following books: *Meditation Is Life; Life Is Meditation* which provides information in depth and detail. *Breath of Love* and *Moving Dhamma Volume Vol. 1* also offers skillful guidance as one goes deeper into the practice. These are all written by Venerable Bhante Vimalaraṁsi.

My purpose here is to put down on paper the steps to awakening — the progress through the levels of insight to awakening. It is my hope that this knowledge can be handed down, studied in the future, and not lost. This book is based on Venerable Bhante Vimalaraṁsi's sutta-based methods and results, using texts from his various talks as well drawing on my own personal experiences involving this practice.

Today's practices include Brahminic influences, New Age methods, and even a new take on Buddhism in which the Buddha himself starts to disappear from the pages. This is called Secular Buddhism or just Mindfulness, with no mention of the Buddha. The *heartwood* of the Buddha's teachings has been mixed up with Western psychology, and even the word Mindfulness is no longer being used in the way the Buddha intended.

An important goal of this book is to show how Buddhism, as it is generally taught today, has veered away from the ideas presented in the suttas. It has deviated from what the historical Buddha taught.

We are going to explore, among other things:

- What the Buddha taught us in his own words from the suttas

- Awakening both Mind and Body

- Dependent Origination

- The Definition of Mindfulness

- What is Tranquil Wisdom Insight Meditation (TWIM)

- What are the 6 Rs?

- Two types of Jhānas: Absorption Jhānas and Aware Jhānas

- The Progress through the Jhānas to Nibbāna

- The Four stages of Sainthood

Chapter One: What Is Buddhism?

Around 2,600 years ago, when the young Prince Siddhartha Gautama went outside his palace into the village, he realized suffering was experienced universally by all beings. He found that there was sickness, old age, and death and it so shocked him that he left behind his wife and newborn son, his kingdom, and all his worldly goods to go in search of a way to end this suffering. After years of searching, he finally discovered the path to the end of suffering — Nibbāna — a path which he described as not only achieving release from suffering but that it was also "immediately effective" or not taking that long if practiced correctly. He then spent the next forty-five years teaching that path to others. During that time many people were awakened.

The Mahāvacchagotta Sutta, number 73 in the Majjhima Nikāya (MN), confirms and gives us more details about just how many thousands of people were awakened. In the sutta, when the Buddha is asked if there were any beings who had been successful, he clearly described the numbers and attainments of those he had taught.

What is suffering? The Buddha stated the cause through his Four Noble Truths:

- There are suffering and dissatisfaction in the world and in our lives.

- The cause and origin of that suffering is *craving*.

- The *cessation of craving* is the cessation of suffering.

- The eightfold path leads us to the end of that suffering.

This is Buddhism in brief: suffering, the *cause* of suffering, the *end* of suffering, and the *path* leading to the end of suffering. This is the heart of Buddhism. It is not about rites and rituals, prayers, and incense. It is not a *religion,* but a scientific investigation into overcoming sorrow at all levels of mind and body.

In modern times, it seems that few people actually reach awakening. Some teachers explain that people in the Buddha's time were more spiritually developed and some say it was because of the Buddha himself. Others attribute the lack of success to the so-called darker times in which we now live. But the Buddha made it clear that if you follow the directions, awakening can be achieved in a single lifetime, even in as little as a few days. This is as true today as it was at the time of the Buddha. This book just might be the proof.

People are different culturally, but our minds and bodies all function in the same way. This means that if we follow the true path of the Buddha, we too can experience awakening in a short period of time. The experiences of our students who have followed the instructions from the earliest suttas precisely, without adding or subtracting anything, are proof of that. They have experienced the states I will talk about, and so can you!

A Supra-Mundane Science

Dr. Albert Einstein is attributed to have said that if he were ever interested in getting involved with religion, he would become a Buddhist. Buddhism, he said, is the religion that is the closest to science. He talked about a "cosmic" religion which he felt Buddhism was closer to.

Certainly, most people think of Buddhism as a religion. But what is a religion? Religion is defined in the Merriam-Webster dictionary as follows:

- Belief in a god or a group of gods;
- An organized system of beliefs, ceremonies, and rules used to worship a god or a group of gods

So, is Buddhism a religion? Many sects of Buddhism seem to treat it as such, and certainly, most people consider it one. But the Buddha left out the whole concept of God, and what the Buddha taught is certainly beyond any religious belief system.

Then is it science? Perhaps, but it may even be beyond science — at least the existing level of today's knowledge.

Because the Buddha's concern was with the cause and the cessation of suffering, much of what he taught focused on the development of mind through deep meditative practices.

There is a growing tendency currently in the scientific community to explain everything about mind in terms of neuroscience and the study of the brain. In fact, much of neuroscience sees mind as just a product of the functioning brain. But this is a limited understanding of mind.

So, in one corner, you have practitioners of meditation wanting to find happiness with religious leaders' teachings and meditation, and in the other corner, you have Western scientists wanting to find happiness through the study of the physical brain. There seems to be the goal — maybe hope is a better word — that by understanding the brain we can somehow develop a therapy or pill to attain happiness.

Studying the neural system will give us an idea of how neurons work and what they look like on an MRI and other medical measurement equipment. It may also show us what parts of the brain are used for certain mental functions. But, it will never explain the insights that are experienced by mind. For our purposes, it does not give insights into the true nature of suffering and how, through seeing these insights, Nibbāna can be attained.

There is no way, at least that we know of now, to duplicate the process of awakening in the lab by any physical process (drugs, machines, etc.) To achieve awakening, we must understand, at a very deep level, how body and mind working together is an impersonal process without any self or soul.

The brain is not mind, and mind is not the brain — the brain is just part of the body like an arm or a finger. Mind is something that sits in dependence upon the physical body. However, mind is something we cannot directly measure and can only *indirectly* understand. Why? Because we are dependent on the reported experience of the individual for this information. When studying another person to find out their actual cognition of something, we only have what they tell us. We cannot measure, for example, their understanding of reality.

So, since science is defined by Merriam Webster's dictionary as "systematized knowledge derived from observation, study, and experimentation carried on in order to determine the nature or principles of what is being studied," then saying that Buddhism leans more toward science than belief is close, but still not quite right.

The Buddha did leave us a clear set of methods and instructions that have come down to us from the suttas which allow us to go deeply into our mind and observe things firsthand.

Whenever the Buddha taught the way to the cessation of suffering, he always told his followers that they did not have to believe what he said, but that they should "come and see" for themselves, as he suggested in the Kalama Sutta. Do not take up his teachings with only faith; try it first, and then dismiss it if it has no measurable benefit. No belief or faith was asked for by the Buddha.

These instructions still apply: Try the practice as the Buddha taught it. You decide for yourself if the results you are having are the same as those that are described and if they are beneficial to you. When you see that they work and produce repeatable results, this develops confidence and encourages you to continue on the path.

If we only study the brain, we cannot purport to be studying mind, as mind is only truly knowable by the individual being studied. The researcher must ask the subject what happened. They can never know how understanding and wisdom have internally affected the subject's mind. This is something *beyond* simple science.

When we say that the Buddha's teachings go beyond science (i.e., that it is supra-mundane), we are talking about both the actual methods that the Buddha taught and the results (insights) achieved with the practice. While both the methods and the results are repeatable and measurable, they are also subjective experiences. They are transformative and profound but not easily measured by outside researchers.

The Buddha was not just trying to understand "the nature and principles of what is being studied." He was searching for a way to finally end personal suffering — not just obtain "understanding" of it.

Buddhism is beyond any scientific study because *only by observing mind directly* with one's own consciousness can we *understand* mind. Once the understanding is achieved then that mind being observed is *transformed*.

In India, it is called a "subjective" science. I call it supra-mundane science. This is why we needed a Buddha to show us the path. The answer was not a simple "this or that." It was a subtle recipe, a complex training, to which he gave the name "The Middle Path" — between all extremes.

Awakening Both Mind and Body

Traditionally, Indian Masters believed that enlightenment could be achieved by *controlling* desire, as desire was believed to be the cause of all kinds of suffering.

Practicing initially within this tradition, the Buddha mastered the mind-based practices of yogic, one-pointed absorption concentration. Following that, he spent some long years mastering the body-based austere, ascetic practices of the yogic sadhus. Both efforts were intended to bring desire under control and thereby bring about awakening.

On the one hand, the Brahminic meditation masters believed that they could control desire by controlling mind. By forcing the attention to stay on an object for longer and longer periods of time, it was thought that *craving,* or desire, could be controlled. But it wasn't that craving would be *overcome* — it was that there would arise this all-powerful *controller* of that craving which, by improving self-discipline

and self-control, would be able to exert mastery over desire —
holding it down and keep it from coming up; pushing it down versus
eliminating it.

But then we'd have to ask the question, who is our "real self"
here? The controlling one — the mind that wished to control desire —
or the one with the desire, or neither? For there even to be a self, there
must be something that is considered not the self (or at least not our
real self).

 In the Brahmajāla Sutta, No. 1 of the Digha Nikāya, the Buddha
describes there are 62 views of self! There is *self* watching *self*, "*not-
self*" observing *self*, the *self* observing a *not-self* and on and on. There is
only one "you" but which one is it?

If an alcoholic says, they will give up drinking by exercising their
willpower, then who is the real self? Is it the one who wants to keep
drinking or the one who wants to stop drinking? Which one is the
real you?

On the other hand, if controlling desires with mental self-control
and discipline didn't work then ascetics thought that they could
control desire by controlling the body. Yogis would stand on one leg
for extended periods or eat a very restricted diet, believing that by
controlling the body in this way, enlightenment would surely come.
Mind would experience a breakthrough when the control of the body
was mastered — again, self-discipline would enable someone to take
charge and bring desire under control.

This, "someone," was conceived as the "Higher Self" or the "I"
who would finally have *total control* such that one would *no longer be
subject to desire and its suffering*. This was the perceived goal of the
meditation practice. It wasn't about eliminating desire but actually
controlling desire!

After practicing both approaches extensively, the future Buddha
or *Bodhisatta* had not achieved awakening. When he entered deep
states of absorption concentration, he found that these states
suppressed his sense bases so that he no longer felt, heard, or

experienced anything from the body. The mental states he achieved were blissful and sublime. However, he soon realized that tightly controlling mind did suppress desire, but only while he was practicing. This was temporary. It did not eradicate the craving mind entirely. As soon as he stopped practicing, desire returned in full force.

Similarly, after six years of ascetic practices, when he was about to die from hunger near Bodh Gaya, he understood that excessive controlling of the body through deprivation would only lead to death through starvation. It would not, however, lead to the elimination of desire. The cessation of suffering would never be achieved with these practices.

When he had all but given up practicing concentration meditation and ascetic techniques to their absolute limit, he realized that control was not the answer. It was a futile practice, that didn't lead to awakening, using "craving" to control craving. At that point, he sat down under the Bodhi Tree and determined that he would sit there until he found the answer.

On a full moon day in May, he became the *Tathāgata*, the Buddha, the Awakened One (in the third watch of the night, between 3 and 7 a.m.). He had found the Middle Way. He had come to understand the need to employ a meditation method that used a totally different approach — a method that would include both mind and body and eliminated the *controller*.

The Buddha had previously developed the seeing and understanding of how his mind worked by careful observation. He began to see that the mental processes are a dependent chain of events arising and passing away. We now know this as seeing the *links of dependent origination.* The Buddha used the term *paṭicca samuppāda*, which is Pāli for dependent origination.

On the morning of his awakening, he realized that seeing clearly, the deepest phenomena in mind, is without a doubt, the way to Nibbāna. By seeing how his own mind worked and closely observing the mental processes, he grew to understand that we all cause our own suffering!

He saw how desire works, how it leads to suffering, and how the cessation of suffering can be achieved. The Buddha realized that desires arise because we feed them and continually chase after them. We see them as ours and personally identify with them.

In other words, if you are sitting quietly and your mind goes to thinking about how nice it would be to be somewhere else, can you stop it? Can you just say, "that's ok mind, I'd like to sit quietly and enjoy some peace this afternoon." No — here come the desires for this and that unasked, uncalled for. In that sense, it is not "our" desire.

Because we personally identify with these desires that we experience, thinking of them as "mine," and then become attached to them, this craving inevitably leads to suffering. We have no control over how or when they arise, or how or when they pass away. Craving and suffering occur because we identify with and personalize these desires and then cling to them.

Dependent origination is the understanding that all things in both body and mind are conditioned. They are conditioned or caused by what came before, and they inevitably lead to what happens next. By seeing this chain of events clearly, we see that everything is impersonal. So, where are "we" in this process? Where am "I?"

An important part of understanding dependent origination is that this thing we call "self" or "ego" is actually not a self or ego at all, but an impersonal process that happens completely beyond our control. In fact, there is no possibility of control because there is no continuous or permanent "self" capable of being the controller. The Buddha saw that there are only processes arising and passing away with no permanent self involved.

Who controls anything? Who makes the decisions? Even "decision" itself is another conditioned mental process which arises based on previous actions. Decisions aren't made by some permanent self who has control of what's happening; they are *"the impersonal you"* at that moment. Our only possible input is to recognize the reality of this situation and not to take it personally, not to be "attached" to the outcome of any given situation. This is the practice of "Right Effort" (we call it the 6Rs and will discuss this later). This was a unique and profound truth that the Buddha discovered and presented to the thinkers of his time.

Once the Buddha fully and deeply realized what he had discovered, he found that craving and suffering ceased. And today researchers have found that there are, indeed, measurable changes in both the mind and bodies of meditators as various types of meditation techniques are practiced. There are measurable positive results.

The Buddha realized that he could not break through to awakening by controlling either mind or body independently. You can't turn off input from the body by suppressing the sense bases in some sort of deep concentration. On the other hand, you can't torture the body and expect this to lead to some sort of control of mind (by controlling pain).

The Buddha understood that mind and body worked together, but first, he tried controlling each one *separately,* as far as he could muster his energy and determination.

It didn't work. The result was that he gave up trying to control mind and body to look for another way to solve this dilemma.

Hundreds of years later there came commentaries and opinions about the Buddha's teachings, like the *Visuddhi Magga,* which started to split up practices, fundamentally discriminating *insight* and *concentration* (vipassanā and samatha) into different techniques, whereas the original suttas had called for them to be "yoked together."

The Visuddhi Magga was written in 430 C. E., over 900 years after the Buddha lived. It is a large volume written by Buddhaghosa that attempts to lay out (mostly) the chief meditative practices that the Buddha taught. It is especially considered a very important document for the Theravada Buddhist sect. Since it is not the words of the Buddha, it is considered a commentary on his practices. In the Visuddhi Magga, there are many methods involved in developing concentration. Some use *Kasinās* or colored discs. Many use the breath to create a *nimitta* or sign on which to concentrate. We will describe the origins of the book later and how it fits with meditation practice.

Then came "Dry Insight Practice," which avoided deep concentration entirely. Those teachers even told their practitioners to stay away from concentrated absorption practices because they might get "attached." This Dry Insight method developed only enough concentration to start investigating the mental process, without the benefit of the stronger type of concentration. Teachers of such an approach said it was faster and more direct. The question here is, did the Buddha teach this?

Here is the critical understanding of what the Buddha taught: In the suttas, he says that concentration *(samatha)* is yoked together with insight *(vipassanā)*. Samatha and vipassanā, therefore, must be practiced together.

This is what is actually taught in the suttas, and this is what Bhante Vimalaraṁsi rediscovered hiding there in plain sight — he has named this *Tranquil Wisdom Insight Meditation* or *Aware Jhāna Practice.*

Before we get into meditation practice, let us look at how mind works by examining what the Buddha considered the most important concept to learn.

Dependent Origination — Leaving Control Behind

After years of practice in the Brahminic tradition, on the night of his awakening, the Buddha realized why he had not found relief. The fundamental premise of those practices was incorrect. That idea assumed that one could actually control desire and thereby control suffering. On the night of his awakening, the Buddha directly realized what he had already reasoned out about his own mental processes. He understood that everything has craving in it and arises because of actions that took place in the past. Because those actions have already happened, no one has any control over what will emerge or how they will react to it. In other words, you cannot, in fact, control what desire arises but can only observe the impersonal arising of it.

What is dependent origination and how does it work? When one sits and quiets mind, all becomes still. The next thing that might happen is a sound arising. A bird may chirp. The sound *form* (the chirp) hits the ear base (the organ, physical ear), and ear-consciousness arises. These three things — sound, the ear base, and ear-consciousness — are the *contact* link in the twelve links of dependent origination. *Contact (phassa)* is all three elements coming together so that "hearing" happens.

In the same way, lighting a match, you have the match head, the flammable chemicals and the flint of the matchbox. When they are struck together, this is called contact. Heat and light arise, resulting in a flame. If either one of these three things are missing, "hearing" doesn't happen.

Once hearing happens, there arises a feeling (*vedanā*) associated with that sound; then perception arises that it is pleasant, unpleasant, or neither-pleasant nor unpleasant (neutral). Feeling and perception are followed by craving (*taṇhā*) arising with the formula: "I like it" or "I don't like it" or "I don't care." This is where you start to identify with what is happening and take it personally.

Craving can always be recognized as tension and tightness in the head. The tension or tightness is how you recognize craving. You must see and let go of this craving in the head; that desire is what is next going to lead you into thought (clinging) and then leads to the birth of action and resulting in "sorrow, lamentation, grief, and despair."

Following craving, clinging (*upādāna*) — or thinking — arises, the story about why you like it or don't like it. This is based on your past experience — what happened when that sound arose at some past time. You remember a time when you were bird-watching and heard a unique type of bird. Thoughts arise, and a story begins about the sound.

Then there arises a drive or an urge to action associated with what you might do when that sound is heard. This is the habitual emotional tendency or behavior (*bhava*). For example, if you are a birdwatcher, when you hear a bird, you have a habitual tendency to reach for your camera, or you might have a tendency to reach for your binoculars.

A habitual emotional tendency is something you always tend to do in a certain situation. It can be your habitual reaction to a feeling you have. Someone comes in the room and complains about something. You always react in the same way, by not liking it and emotionally reacting to the person complaining.

Your spouse calls and says he/she will be home late from work — you may get this kind of call quite a bit, and react the same way every time with a negative reaction. It might be a judgment of, "you are unreliable," or it might be a reaction to lash out because you think he/she isn't telling the truth. It is habitual; it tends to come up when this situation occurs.

When this habitual reaction arises, this is where the strong tendency to try and control your feelings with your thoughts arises. You observe that mind is disturbed and you react with frustration, trying to control the disturbing thoughts. This is the start of taking something personally. You become *emotional*.

Mind has many factors or states of consciousness contained in it. There is a greedy mind, and there is a joyful mind. In the Anupada Sutta, the Buddha says that even the mental factor of *decision* is conditioned by previous actions from the past. This decision process is something that you might call a *volition* or *intention,* but we have to be careful to use those words because they might wrongly imply that there is a *self* "making a decision." Decision is just a small, yet the most important factor of the "coming to a decision."

Chapter One: What is Buddhism?

As stated previously, phenomena arise and pass like the sound of a bird, and are dependent on that sound for its existence. When your mind is very tranquil, you can see the decision factor arise as well as the "push" that goes with it to "make the decision." It's pretty interesting when you can observe your mind operating at this level and see how, truly, "you," i.e., "I," am not in charge.

For example, a desire arises to get a cup of tea. You then continue to think about which tea might taste good. If you are very mindful, you can see the exact moment when you "decide" which tea to have.

There is a moment in which "your" decision arises. If you back away gently, just allowing everything to arise, very carefully watching it (this is your mental investigation factor), you will see *the decision (mental) factor* arise entirely on its own. And then it also passes away. There appears this call to action arising through the craving attached to it. This craving is the push you feel to go into action.

Is there really free will? Is there some soul or entity down deep making decisions? *Kind of…* yet at the deepest level, there is only the deciding mind that arises and passes away. So you have the decision there, but it is a conditioned decision.

The phrase "volitional formations" used in the sutta texts is inadequate, not precisely correct. Volition indicates *someone is deciding*, but there is no one there to do that. There are only causes and conditions. There is no "you" that makes the decision, just the deciding moment. The only real power we have is to allow and observe, releasing and relaxing into that decision, seeing it fade away.

Continuing, after the habitual tendency link in dependent origination comes the actual *birth of action (jāti)* link, and you get up to go get your camera. The drive to action translates into taking action. This can be bodily action (moving), verbal action (speaking), or mental action (thinking).

Unfortunately, by the time you get back with your camera, the bird has flown away. Due to the result of your action in getting the camera, dissatisfaction might arise because now the bird is gone. You think your actions always will lead you to what you want, but you can never really positively be sure of the results of any action. The best-laid plans of mice and men…

Then, what follows the *Birth of Action* link is the last link: *Sorrow, Lamentation, Grief, and Despair*. Yes, there are some happy moments here and there, but they are fleeting! Even if you get that picture, you'll wish the bird had stayed longer, or that you'd recorded its song, etc.

In the twelve links of dependent origination, we just went through the last part of the process, the grosser and observable part. These are the last seven: Contact; Feeling; Craving; Clinging; Habitual Tendency; Birth of Action; and Sorrow, Lamentation, Grief, and Despair. These are the ones you can see without having to go too deep into the meditation.

Contact → Feeling → Craving → Clinging → Habitual Tendency → Birth of Action → Sorrow, Lamentation, Grief, and Despair.

The first five links of the full twelve links of D.O. come before the ones listed above and can be understood as potentials. They can only be observed as subtle movements in mind with the exception of ignorance which is your understanding. Later, when your meditation goes deeper, you will see the arising of the first five: *Ignorance → Formations → Consciousness →Mentality-Materiality →* and the *Sixfold Sense Base*.

The Buddha said that it all starts with ignorance of how things work; that is, ignorance of the truth of dependent origination, and of the Four Noble Truths, which makes clear that craving drives the whole process of suffering. It is this "ignoring" of the Four Noble Truths which leads us to act in unwholesome ways, which creates endless suffering.

On the next page is a chart that shows the circle of dependent origination. Each link is dependent on the link before it as nutriment, as food. In each link, there is also a small additional amount of craving which makes the whole process continue forward in a never-ending chain of events.

The Samyutta Nikāya has a wealth of information about Dependent Origination and what it is. Here are the basics.

SN 12.1. "Monks, I will teach you dependent origination. Listen to that and attend closely, I will speak."–"Yes, venerable sir," those monks replied. The Blessed One said this:

"And what, monks, is dependent origination? With ignorance as condition, formations come to be; with formations as condition, consciousness; with consciousness as condition, name-and-form; with name-and-form as condition, the six sense bases; with the six sense bases as condition, contact; with contact as condition, feeling; with feeling as condition, craving; with craving as condition, clinging; with clinging as condition, existence; with existence as condition, birth; with birth as condition, aging-and-death, sorrow, lamentation, pain, displeasure, and despair come to be. Such is the origin of this whole mass of suffering. This, monks, is called dependent origination.

"But with the remainderless fading away and cessation of ignorance comes cessation of formations; with the cessation of formations, cessation of consciousness; with the cessation of consciousness, cessation of name-and-form; with the cessation of name-and-form, cessation of the six sense bases; with the cessation of the six sense bases, cessation of contact; with the cessation of contact, cessation of feeling; with the cessation of feeling, cessation of craving; with the cessation of craving, cessation of clinging; with the cessation of clinging, cessation of existence; with the cessation of existence, cessation of birth; with the cessation of birth, aging-and-death, sorrow, lamentation, pain, displeasure, and despair cease. Such is the cessation of this whole mass of suffering."

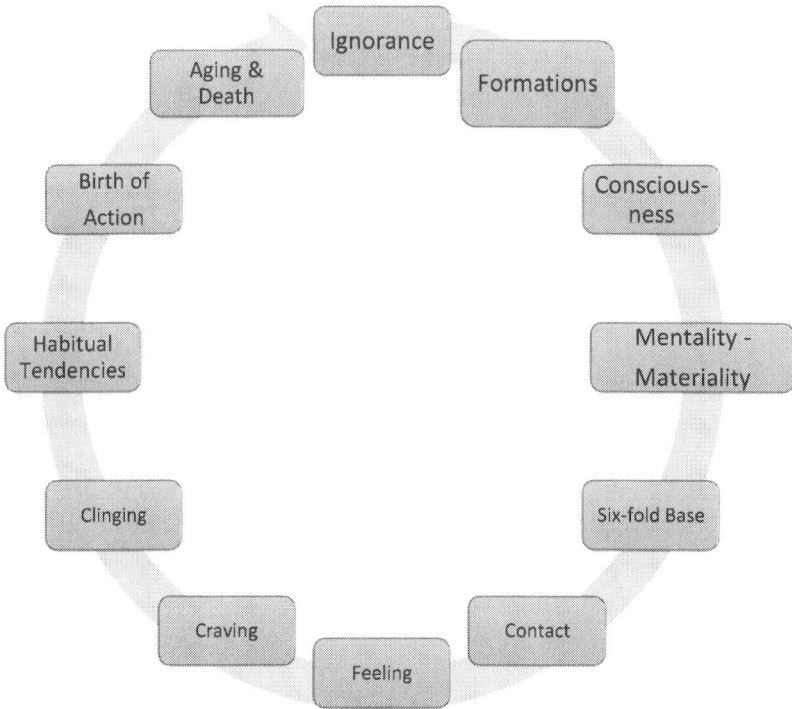

The highest goal of TWIM is to see how each link is dependent on or conditioned by the previous link. When one understands this process in a deep and profound way, the unconditioned state, Nibbāna, arises for the first time. This first instance is the Path Knowledge. One realizes that there is no personal self or ego, just an impersonal process dependent on conditions.

From this realization comes tremendous relief, because, as the famous Zen saying goes, "No self, no problem!" No one is there, so nobody to control.

It's as if we see a dark figure walking toward us; fear might arise because our mind throws up this concept of a villain from our past, yet when we get closer we see it is our friend and that fearful image is replaced by another happy image. Just in the same way, we thought there was a self there, and now we see that it was an illusion.

We can follow the links of dependent origination in our own behavior in much the same way we look at a town and trace it back over the last hundred years. The first buildings led to more buildings, then they deteriorated and were replaced by different buildings, and so on and so forth. This arising and passing away of conditions is like the arising and passing away of a great city, flourishing and deteriorating, and constantly changing. Finally, it disappears because of countless causes depending on each other. There is no controller making decisions and taking actions there in that city. There are only changes occurring, conditioned by what has happened in the past.

Similarly, you have no personal self or soul controlling your progress through life. There are only changes that happen due to causes and conditions arising and passing away. This is what we mistakenly call our self — me, myself, and I. It's an impersonal process, an endless chain of causes and conditions that flow like a river; a river that we mistakenly take as ourselves.

Dependent Origination is, indeed, the most important principle of Buddhism along with the four noble truths. Understanding the source of suffering is craving and how dependent origination works leads to the elimination of that craving. Understanding that the noble eightfold path is the way to this goal is the heart of Buddhist meditation.

8 Fold Path	
Harmonious Perspective	Right View (Understanding)
Harmonious Imaging	Right Thought
Harmonious Communication	Right Speech
Harmonious Movement	Right Action
Harmonious Life Style	Right Livelihood
Harmonious Practice	Right Effort
Harmonious Observation	Right Mindfulness
Harmonious Collectedness	Right Concentration

Chapter Two: Mindfulness Re-Defined

What is Mindfulness?

Just what does mindfulness mean? There was an article in a Buddhist Magazine where this question was posed to four meditation teachers. By the end of the discussion, a satisfactory answer still had not been reached. They decided to take it up again in next month's magazine!

Mindfulness does seem to be all the rage these days and has gone from its strict Buddhist origins to a more general acceptance anywhere from use by psychologists to children and even by the military. It even has its own magazine: "Mindful." Mindfulness is used to be aware of one's thoughts and one's general state of being and is used to calm one down and relax. These are all good uses, but is it what the Buddha taught? Is the actual procedure of mindfulness being taught today the process he intended.

I have a theory, and you won't find it anywhere else, so please bear with me. The Pāli word for mindfulness is *sati*. When the Pāli texts were translated, the translators ran into this word sati and had to pick out an appropriate English word to translate it to. The problem is that some of the things the Buddha taught were brand new ideas and never had been exposed to European culture. There never were any English words that represented these Eastern concepts. Buddhism had never come to the West. Thus no English vocabulary had been developed.

So what to do? Pick the closest word. *Sati* had to do with observation and to know what was happening, so the word *mindful* was selected. Made sense, but did it?

The problem was that mindfulness already was a solid concept in the English language. "Be mindful of the opening and don't bump your head!" That sort of definition became applied to sati, and thus, to be mindful meant to remember to look where you are going *and* watch carefully the process of getting there.

What happened here is that the English word has exerted powerful undue influence over the Pāli term. Now it was almost as if the Pāli term was created to represent the English word and not the other way around! The Pāli term, in a sense, became the English term.

Because the translators were not meditators, they could only guess what *sati* really meant. That would be fine if that is how *sati* is defined and used in the suttas — but it may not be!

You are now going to get a new definition of the word Mindfulness that is quite different in its application. When tested against the sutta texts you will see that it works better.

The definition of Mindfulness is remembering to observe how mind's attention moves from one thing to another.

Looking closer at this definition the first part is just *remembering,* which sounds easy but it isn't. Once you pay attention, you'll find that your mind is constantly distracted from observation of itself by thoughts over which you have no control. You are aware of mind, a thought arises, and you are pulled away into that thought until you remember that you're supposed to be paying attention to the movement of mind's attention. You bring your observation back to mind, and then maybe a few seconds or minutes later, another thought pulls your attention away.

It's important to remember what it is you're supposed to be doing: observing the process of mind's attention and its movements as part of an impersonal process which leads us to the second part.

On retreat, you go for a walking meditation. As you start your practice and you slowly walk down the path, your mind wanders.

Chapter Two: Mindfulness Re-Defined?

The first thing you must do is to *remember to be mindful*. Then actually *do it!*

So the second part of mindfulness means to become aware of how mind's attention moves from one thing to another. The Buddha intended that the meditator be mindful of what arises in the present, whatever that may be, and that they specifically see how it arises. He didn't care what the feelings or sensations were or whether we peered at them that closely or not, only to know they had arisen. He did not intend for the meditator to pick out specific parts of the four foundations of mindfulness, or the five aggregates of mind and body, and only observe those. That would have been a concentration practice — focusing in on those individual parts.

Rather, he wanted you to watch the activity of mind's attention and to observe: (1) how it arises and passes away without any control on your part, and (2) how you take this mental movement personally as your "self." Mind clamps onto a feeling and then identifies it as "my" feeling even though you did not ask for it to arise, or to pass away. You never had any control over it whatsoever. It just arose when conditions were right.

This identification with feeling gives rise to a false belief in a personal self — the concept of "I." When you see how the "I" concept arises, you can release it by not keeping attention on it, relax the tension or tightness caused by that disturbance, smile into it, and return to the meditation object; it becomes clear that there never was a self at all. There is only the endless stream of activity.

Since you have no control over what comes up, you begin to see how this identification process — craving — is at the root of suffering. Craving manifests as that desire to control what happens. And when even that can't be accomplished, suffering arises, and we don't like it. This leads to frustration and an even further desire to control.

So again, what is the definition of mindfulness? Mindfulness is remembering to observe how mind's attention moves from one thing to another, as things arise unasked and they then completely pass away when they have run their course.

Mindfulness is not over-focusing on an object — feeling or breath or anything else — it only **knows** that it is happening.

This process of observing the movement of mind's attention is where you see the hindrances arise and pull your attention away.

There are five hindrances:

1. *Greed or sensual desires*

2. *Hatred or aversion*

3. *Sloth (laziness/sleepy) and torpor (dullness)*

4. *Restlessness, worry, or anxiety*

5. *Doubt (in yourself, the teacher, the practice, or the Buddha)*

As you stay with your object of meditation, this is where you will find craving rearing its ugly head. It is your goal to fully understand how craving arises, and by understanding the process, you let go of this craving and stay with the object of meditation. And you don't do this by clenching your teeth and pushing it away.

You want to make the hindrances your friends. They are your teachers. They show you where you are attached. When you fully understand them, you will need no more instruction. You will graduate to awakening! You will see the four foundations of mindfulness with pure, clear observation power. You will see them free of craving and free of your taking them personally. It will be a relief to give up the control of those things that are uncontrollable!

The Four Foundations of Mindfulness

As we investigate deeper into TWIM Meditation, it is important to understand the *Four Foundations of Mindfulness* and how they are correctly applied to the meditation practice.

MN 10, the Satipaṭṭhāna Sutta, tells us to observe the four foundations of mindfulness. The sutta says to observe the four foundations and let go of craving and clinging — letting go of taking the foundations *personally*.

The Four Foundations are Body, Feeling, Mind, and Mind Objects. They are also known as the Five Aggregates: Body, Feeling, Perception, Formations, and Consciousness.

When the Four Foundations are used instead of the Five Aggregates, Perception and Feeling are joined together. The Four Foundations and the Five Aggregates are different ways of saying the same thing, but it depends on whether you are talking about meditation or talking about the impersonal process of the existence of mind and body.

We want to see what is there before we create confusion by identifying with what we are observing and taking it as our "self." We want to see the body only as a body, feeling only as feeling, consciousness only as consciousness, and so forth. We need to observe impersonality or *anattā* for ourselves.

The Visuddhi Magga explains that the Satipaṭṭhāna sutta methodology is to break up these four foundations and practice them separately. If you want to observe the body, then only observe the breath (part of the body). If you want to observe feeling, then only observe feeling, and so on.

The Vipassanā Insight Meditation practice breaks up the four foundations as described above. You observe and focus in on just one of them separately. For the most part, you watch breath going in and out, but some teachers will try to explain that you have to watch feeling or mind objects separately in a different iteration of the practice. As you focus in on feeling, for example, you only see feeling and not the rest of the aggregates that go with it. You are not truly mindful which means to see how your attention moves from one thing to another. It isn't to just look at the objects themselves in a concentrated way but the relationship between the object of meditation and the other objects moving around it.

That explanation is not what is in the suttas. You don't break the four up. You can't. You observe all foundations because they all occur together. All of the foundations exist in every moment, or you would not exist. You cannot have body arise without feeling it, perceiving it, and cognizing it. You can't have a mind with no mind objects, body or feelings.

The foundations arise and are observed as being conjoined. They are not separate things. We have a mind and a body dependent on each other, clearly observable in even the earliest stages of the meditation. You can't observe body without consciousness or perception to cognize what is there, or without feeling to know what feeling is there in the body. It is like disassembling a car down to its parts and observing it running — it can't be observed in operation without all its parts assembled and running together.

Feeling Is Not Feelings

Let's stop here for a minute and talk about the feeling foundation. To be clear, we are talking about *feeling*, not feelings. In the suttas the aggregate of feeling (*vedanā*) is without the "s;" it is just sensation with a feeling "tone" to it. Just feeling itself, that's all. The most important part of this feeling is that it is either a pleasant feeling, painful feeling, or neither pleasant nor painful feeling.

"Feelings," on the other hand, are usually understood to be emotional states which mean there is craving mixed in. If you look at someone whom you find attractive, and a pleasant feeling comes up, lust likely will arise. A pleasant feeling with lust ("I like it") is what we call "emotions" (*habitual tendency — bhava*). That emotion might be categorized as a pleasant feeling or desire that is taken personally. This feeling with the personalization is commonly known as *feelings* with an "*s*" on the end.

For example, "Love," where referred to romantically, is not loving-kindness. This kind of love in a relationship is much more related to the state of affection, or infatuation, and has craving in it.

Chapter Two: Mindfulness Re-Defined?

Loving-kindness is a pure, non-personal state – a true wish for someone to be happy. Loving-kindness may turn into compassion when it is directed toward someone who is suffering. It doesn't turn into hatred or sadness. It's never taken personally. These are not "feelings," they are just feeling.

The Buddha considered *feeling* to be anything that was felt; in other words, he considered feeling as any mental or physical experience that was felt. He categorized feeling as either pleasant, unpleasant or neither-pleasant-nor-unpleasant (neutral). He did *not* use the word sensation here. He did not care whether it was a feeling of heat or a feeling of hardness or the taste of a mango or a banana flavor. He only wanted you to consider whether it was pleasant, unpleasant or neutral; no need to dive deeper.

Why is this distinction important? Why, because feeling leads to craving. The "I like it" or "I don't like it" states of craving are dependent on feeling and will arise in the untrained mind if not released quickly. The "I like it" mind may lead to thoughts about why you like it, when you last had it, and when you will get it again. With this process, your mind starts to wander away from your object of meditation.

This is the unwholesome mind in which you are watching the five aggregates arise. It becomes muddy with craving leading to thinking and stories. How do we let go of this craving process and what is a clear mind free of craving?

In the next chapter, we will look at what this freed state is and how it arises. We will consider the stages of progress in the meditation that the Buddha called the jhānas. We will examine what they are using the suttas only — and how, as time passed, the original meaning of this word became confused.

Chapter Three: What Is a Jhāna?

More than One Type of Jhāna

If you have ever run across the word jhāna before, then, it is likely a state that you desire to experience. Jhānas are described as levels of concentration. Contained in them can be bliss and deep contentment which, of course, everyone wants. They are important to understand because the suttas explain that you pass through them on the way to Nibbāna. They *are* the road to Nibbāna.

Actually, there are *two* types of Jhāna!

Today there are so many methods that are taught in meditation practice. Which is right? How can we find out what the Buddha really taught? In the Digha Nikāya, this same dilemma was addressed by the Buddha.

Digha Nikāya Sutta 21. "Sakka asked the Lord: "Sir, do all teachers and Brahmins teach the same Dhamma, practice the same discipline, desire the same thing and pursue the same goal?"

"No, Ruler of the Gods, they do not. And why not? This world is made up of many and various elements, and people adhere to one or another of these elements, and become tenaciously attached to them, saying: 'This alone is true, all else is false.' Therefore, all teachers and Brahmins do not teach the same Dhamma, practice the same discipline, desire the same thing or pursue the same goal."

In this book, we will try to remain faithful to the sutta material as we explain the differences in the many techniques of the Buddhist Universe.

Yes — there are two types of Jhānas and two major types of meditation practice by which to attain those two types of jhāna.

There is the One-Pointed Concentration Absorption practice and the Tranquil Wisdom Insight Meditation (TWIM) practice.

Later, the first type, one-pointed concentration practice, will be broken further into 1) Straight Concentration-Absorption practice 2) Concentration-Absorption Insight Practice and 3) Dry Insight practice.

The Pāli word *jhāna* was not used in reference to meditation prior to the Buddha. The Buddha did use it to describe his own experiences during meditation practice.

While the Pāli word jhāna is often translated as a state of "concentration," this is not correct from the viewpoint of TWIM. Pāli experts like Most Venerable Punnaji of Malaysia say that *jhāna* just means "level." If you check a Pāli dictionary, it also defines it as "meditation" or "state of meditation."

Most Venerable Punnaji also offers an alternate definition of the related word *samādhi*, which is often considered and used to define a state of absorption concentration. The Pāli word *sama* means "equal or even;" *dhi* means "state" in this usage. So, Most Venerable Punnaji translates *samādhi* as "an even state of balance." The word *samādhi* implies a collected and unified state, but not deep absorption that suppresses the hindrances. It is a more open and aware state.

Venerable Bhante Vimalaraṁsi defines the word *jhāna* as "a level of understanding." Each successive jhāna is an increasingly deeper level of understanding of the workings of dependent origination and the mental process. Bhante Vimalaraṁsi uses "collectedness" to translate the word concentration more accurately.

Additionally, Bhante has found that in Pāli that the word *dhi* may also be translated as "wisdom" in terms of the levels of understanding. Thus, we put together *sama* and *dhi* resulting in "Tranquil Wisdom."

Chapter Three: What is Jhāna?

In the Buddha's description of the jhānas, as you go deeper into the practice, the attainment of each jhāna reflects a deeper level of understanding of what it means to let go of craving. You pass through the jhānas as you progress from gross craving to a finer and finer balance of mind until finally, after the state of *neither-perception-nor-non-perception*, the highest jhāna, you reach the cessation of craving. This is the gateway to the attainment of Nibbāna. At that moment, the cessation of craving (*nirodha samāpatti*) occurs. This is the state of no feeling, no perception, and no consciousness arising at all. The mind just stops, and Nibbāna arises.

Again, *jhāna* never was supposed to mean "absorption." It means a collected state or a level of understanding in mental development. However, as emphasis shifted away from the Buddha's actual teachings as described in the suttas, to the commentaries like the Visuddhi Magga, the word *jhāna* was more commonly used to describe the state of one-pointed concentration.

In the Anguttara Nikāya, the book of fives, number 27 we have this quote:

AN 5. 27. "…The knowledge arises that is personally yours: 'This concentration is peaceful and sublime, gained by full tranquiliza-tion, and attained to unification; it is not reined in and checked by forcefully suppressing the defilements…"

Clearly, this quote indicates an open and aware state and not an absorbed suppressing state.

So there are two kinds of jhāna or two different ways to understand the term. One style is made up of *one-pointed absorption jhānas*, which are achievable by various concentration methods, including observing the breath, focusing on a colored disc (*kasinā*), or absorbing yourself in a candle flame. These jhānas are the states achieved by the yogic masters and were learned by the future Buddha when he first started down the path.

The absorption concentration jhānas have been adopted by many of today's Buddhist monks and are supported by commentaries like the Visuddhi Magga.

Ven. Bhante Vimalaraṁsi explains,

"The Visuddhi Magga was written by Venerable Buddhaghosa Acariya in the fifth century, one thousand years after the Buddha died. Buddhaghosa was asked by his teacher to go to Sri Lanka and translate the commentaries written in Sinhalese back into the Pāli language for a readable translation.

"Venerable Buddhaghosa also had the task of bringing four different sects of Buddhism together so all of the different sects would stop arguing. He was a very good student of the Pāli language, a true scholar, but he didn't study the suttas. He didn't practice meditation himself. Before he became a Buddhist monk, he was a Sanskrit scholar who had memorized all the Vedas, the ancient Brahmin texts.

"Unfortunately, because the author wasn't a practitioner of meditation, he relied heavily on what was in other commentaries for his information about how to do the meditation. He mistakenly divided and pulled apart the Buddha's teaching into two separate types of practice: Concentration or Samatha, and Insight or Vipassanā. The suttas, on the other hand, will always talk about Samatha-Vipassanā being yoked together.

"Nevertheless, the Visuddhi Magga today, more than the suttas, is considered as the encyclopedia of meditation for Buddhism and has become the basic instructions for the entire system of Theravada Buddhism. It is the 'Bible,' and textbook for how to practice."

One of Venerable Bhante Vimalaraṁsi's teachers told him that to be a Theravada monk; he must subscribe to everything in the Visuddhi Magga. Bhante reflected for a moment and said, "I guess I am not a Theravada monk; I am a Buddhist monk." Even though he used some of the advice in the Visuddhi Magga, he couldn't go along with all of it because of the many contradictions and discrepancies with the suttas.

In MN 36, "Mahāsaccaka Sutta," the Buddha says that he tried concentration-absorption practice and rejected it as not being the way to awakening. This is why we, who are following the suttas, cannot say that we are truly Theravāda. We call ourselves "Suttavāda" (following only the sutta texts) or just plain Buddhists!

The second type of jhana is the *Tranquil Aware Jhāna*, which is the jhāna described in the suttas. Bhante Vimalaraṁsi *rediscovered* these when he studied what had been written texts. By practicing from the sutta texts, Bhante found a step-by-step diminishing of craving while progressing through the tranquil aware jhanas, as it is described in sutta MN 111, the Anupada Sutta.

It is helpful to understand that the jhana factors — these are the wholesome states that arise when one is in jhāna — in a tranquil aware jhāna or in an absorption concentration jhāna are very similar in nature. The difference is that in a tranquil aware jhāna the hindrances are gently released, and in the concentration state the hindrances are suppressed and pushed aside. The resulting states that arise are similar but definitely not the same.

The chief characteristic of the first jhāna is joy; the second jhāna, deeper joy and confidence; the third jhāna, happiness and contentment; and the fourth jhāna, very deep balance and equanimity.

What is confusing is that both concentration-absorption jhānas *and* tranquil aware jhānas both have.these same qualities. They manifest differently however in each of the two types of jhāna. In the absorption type, they are more pronounced and very intense. In the Aware Jhāna, they are more balanced with more equanimity and not as extreme.

The fourth jhāna is further split into four bases: the Base of Infinite Space, which has the feeling of expansion; the Base of Infinite

Consciousness, in which consciousness is seen in its infinite arising and passing away; the Base of Nothingness, in which there is a feeling that there is nothing; and the Base of Neither-Perception-Nor-Non-Perception in which mind is barely noticed at all. Later we will investigate these further.

The fact that similar yet different states arise in both the absorption and aware jhānas speaks to the confusion about the two types of jhānas. How can there be two different jhāna types that have similar characteristics but are attained with different techniques? No wonder after 2500+ years things have become murky.

Before we look at the sutta texts regarding the jhānas, let's look more deeply at how the two types are generally taught. We'll start with one-pointed absorption jhānas.

Concentration Absorption Jhāna

Absorption is attained through the powerful concentration of one's mind on a single object, ignoring and pushing any distraction that pulls mind's attention away. One-pointed concentration jhāna is the so-called yogic state where one reaches a level of absorption in which they have no sense of the outside world. You do not hear or feel anything, and you are only aware of mind. The concentration absorption states are deep and can take years of practice and discipline to achieve.

The meditator is constantly reminded to bring his mind back to his object if it wanders away. You might pull it back, and sometimes you end up pushing so hard you "jerk" it back to the object. There is no real letting go and allowing, soft or hard, forcing of mind to stay with the object.

With the absorption jhānas, the Visuddhi Magga explains the preliminary state of concentration is called *upacāra* or access concentration; you are still aware and not yet absorbed fully (Note that this term or idea doesn't appear in the suttas!).

In this access concentration, no hindrance will stick in your mind. Even if you try to bring something up like a thought of anger or lust, it will not stay, and your mind will be clear. Your mind doesn't wander but just rejects any distraction taking it away from its object of meditation. By practicing this pushing away, mind learns to come back to the home object automatically.

As you progress, you will enter full absorption or *appaṇā* concentration, in which awareness of the outside world will disappear entirely. You will have attained the first concentration jhāna level. You then work through the rest of the eight jhānas, using the power of the deep concentration to suppress any further hindrances that arise.

This process *does* work — you do experience concentration states that have similar characteristics to the aware (TWIM) jhānas. But they are *not* the same and have subtle differences which most just dismiss as not important, yet they are. One has some craving left, and one doesn't.

This type of jhāna practice may take over a decade in the Thai tradition to develop. The Sri Lankans say they are better and can get you to the first jhāna in less than ten years of practice. Some others say much less, but it takes an incredible effort.

 Bhante tells a story about a monk who was asked to go into an absorption jhāna, which he did. The monks who were with him picked up his arm and raised it up above his head. It stayed there just hanging in the air. They asked the monk later if he knew they had done this, and he said no. The meditating monk was completely unaware of his body at that time and was only aware of his object of meditation.

When one is absorbed, one cannot hear sounds, feel anything in the body, or sense anything at the physical five senses — so desire at the physical level is suppressed because it isn't there. In addition, because one is so tightly focused on their object of meditation, desire is also suppressed at the mental level. At the fourth absorption jhāna and higher, it is said that the meditator even stops breathing through his mouth and nose, and "breathes" through his ears (This is *not* the case with the Tranquil Aware jhāna, in which one is aware of the outside world and continues to breathe normally).

The Tranquil Aware Jhāna

In MN 26, "The Noble Search," and MN 36, "The Greater Discourse to Saccaka," the Buddha describes his path to awakening. As mentioned in the previous section, he initially believed that the problem of reaching enlightenment was about *control* — controlling mind with the goal to control desire and thus end suffering.

The suttas go on to describe, in some detail, how the Buddha first tried meditation as the primary way to end suffering. He sought out and studied with the most skilled Indian yogic masters of the time, learning everything they had to teach. He initially trained with the absorption jhānas as most yogis were doing at the time.

When Gautama had attained to the seventh absorption jhāna, the state of *Nothingness*, his teacher Ālāra Kalama honored him, saying he had learned everything he had to teach. He invited him to stay and teach at his side. Gautama declined, for he knew there was more left to do. He saw that he could go deeper. There was something more than even this very sublime level of meditation. Suffering still existed. Craving was not yet extinguished.

So, he asked Ālāra Kālāma if there might be an even higher state. Ālāra Kalama told Gautama he knew someone who taught the highest state attainable.

He was told to go study with Uddaka Rāmaputta, who taught him up to attain the eighth absorption jhāna, that of neither-perception-nor-non-perception. He mastered this state in a short time and then the same thing happened. This teacher also invited him to stay and teach. Again, Gautama refused, feeling there was still something more to learn, that this was not the way to Nibbāna.[ii] He still experienced subtle craving after coming out of these high states.

Chapter Three: What is Jhāna?

Once more he left, having been told there was nothing left to be learned. He had mastered the highest yogic state taught at that time. He could find no one else to teach him any higher technique to control his mind.

Venerable Bhikkhu K. Ñāṇananda states in his small book *Nibbāna — The Mind Stilled*, Vol. 2 in sermon 6, p. 127:

"These subtler layers of preparations (thoughts/formations) also have ignorance (craving) hidden within them. That is why…even Āḷāra Kālāma and Uddaka Rāmaputta thought that they could get out of this wheel of existence (saṃsāra) by tranquilizing the bodily activities, the verbal activities, and the mental activities. But they did not understand that all these are saṅkhāras or preparations; therefore, they were confronted with a certain dilemma. They went on calming down the bodily activities to subtler and subtler levels. They calmed down the in-breaths and out breaths, they managed to suppress thinking and pondering by concentration exercises, but without proper understanding. It was only a temporary calming down."

No awakening had yet occurred for Gautama into the true nature of mind, so, disappointed, he rejected all mental absorption-concentration practices and set off to do the austere ascetic practices of the yogic sadhus. By controlling pain in the body through engaging in tortuous, pain-producing practices, he hoped to achieve control of his mind. This would hopefully bring him to peace and a balanced mind.

After six years of austerities, doing unspeakably difficult and even disgusting practices, like drinking his own urine and worse (see suttas MN 36 and MN 12), when he was on the verge of death, the Bodhisatta (the future Buddha) gave up that path as well. He did master control of his body and perfected any austerity that was asked of him, but this did not lead him to the end of desire.

After spending all this time mastering the yogic concentration jhānas and the yogic austerities, the future Buddha sat on the banks of the Ganges, near present-day Bodh Gaya. He was nearly starving to death, down to eating one rice grain per day. He knew he would die if he continued.

A young woman named Sujata came and offered him sweet milk rice to eat. For the first time in a long time, he allowed himself to consume a reasonable portion of food. Immediately, he felt his energy returning. Vitality started to course through his body and mind.

As he sat there on the river's bank, in the shade of a Bodhi tree, he reflected on his past efforts, realizing they had all been in vain. He was no closer to the end of suffering than when he started. He had tried and mastered all of the practices of concentration and austerities and hadn't gotten any closer to awakening.

Then Gautama, the future Buddha, began to reflect on the plight of human beings. In the Saṃyutta Nikāya, the Book of Causation (Niddānnavagga [Origination]),[iii] it says:

> "*Bhikkhus, before my awakening, while I was still a Bodhisatta not yet fully awakened, it occurred to me: Alas, this world has fallen into trouble, in that it is born, ages, and dies, it passes away and is reborn, yet it does not understand the escape from suffering [headed by] aging and death.*
>
> "*Then it occurred to me: 'When what exists does aging, and death come to be? By what is aging and death conditioned?'...there took place in me a breakthrough by wisdom: When there is birth, aging-and-death comes to be: aging-and-death has birth [of action] as its condition.*"

Then it goes on to explain how the Bodhisatta discovered each of the links of dependent origination through reasoning them out. He saw how each link ceased and if that link ceased then the link that followed also ceased. Following the cessation of the last link of ignorance, then the unconditioned arose, Nibbāna.

Chapter Three: What is Jhāna?

Then the Bodhisatta had a memory arise from a time when he was a young boy. He had been left by himself on a sofa under a Roseapple tree while his father, the king, was at the plowshare festival.

He remembered as he became completely tranquil and relaxed, he naturally had fallen into a very peaceful and energetic state, where his mind let go of all hindrances and desires. He entered a completely wholesome, joyful state.

Fully observant and aware, a special tranquil state had arisen. He had let go of all striving at that moment and just observed what was happening; he just let everything be and relaxed even further into it. This was the state the Buddha would later refer to with the Pāli word *Jhāna*.

As the future Buddha sat beneath the Bodhi tree and reflected on this childhood memory, he realized that this was a different kind of state. As he contemplated this condition of mind, he entered this state again naturally.

By completely relaxing both body and mind without trying or controlling, just being there in the present, content and joyful as he had been as a young boy, he achieved the same tranquil, open, and light-minded state. What the Buddha-to-be had found were what Bhante Vimalaraṁsi calls the *Tranquil Aware Jhānas*. This was different from the concentration states he had practiced with his teachers before and it can accurately be more described as a state of *collectedness*.

Collectedness is defined in English as "the state of being calm and composed: "he is the very picture of collectedness and confidence" (Webster's dictionary).

Then he went even deeper. And in the third watch of the night (from 3 a.m. to 7 a.m.), he became the Buddha.

"Buddha" is a title for a fully awakened one. This is not his name, but rather his title. After all, Buddha Gautama was not the first Buddha, nor will he be the last.

I did once have the experience of going into a concentration jhāna, by accident, ironically (wasn't following instructions — typical!), on a TWIM retreat with Bhante Vimalaraṁsi. When I came out, there was a very high, powerful state of awareness with a lot of happiness. It was interesting because it felt very "holy" or sacred and secluded, very much as what I envisioned a "holy" monk would feel. It dissipated in about an hour and just faded away.

The next day it was completely gone, and it felt like nothing had been gained at all by having the experience. I felt empty, in fact, at having gained nothing from such a powerful experience. It was strange that something so potent had no effect on my personality. I wanted to believe otherwise, but really no positive change had taken place. This was an insight to me. I went back and reviewed the instructions again and found that I hadn't been mindful enough. I had let myself become absorbed in the object.

On another TWIM retreat, I purposefully did the breathing meditation using concentration to focus on the breath at the belly, in the way I had done doing Vipassanā. I found a very different experience happened when I forced mind to stay on the breath. Mind became very concentrated. I saw what looked like a border of lights, like a window frame, as if I was looking out a porthole on a ship. There was absolutely nothing inside this ring; just void and silence.

Yet when I came out of that state, I did not feel the same clarity of the TWIM method. The deep concentration left a kind of torpor-like state and was rather uncomfortable. The mind did not feel bright and balanced. It had lost its pliancy and ability to think clearly. Strangely, it felt a little like I was stressed out, jumpy. I went to the Dhamma Talk, and it was a bit hard to follow the talk. Gradually, however, mind returned back to a more balanced state.

With the TWIM meditation, you start by establishing an easy, open, light-minded state. This is accomplished by using the feeling of mettā or loving-kindness as the object of meditation, and by smiling. Radiating mettā outward keeps our attention light and open, while smiling is a wholesome movement that keeps us from taking the meditation too seriously, thereby creating tension and tightness (or, as the suttas call it, craving). We prefer the loving-kindness object as it leads to faster progress, but breath can also be used if we employ the relax step properly. Below we will use the Satipaṭṭhāna Sutta to understand the meditation process in terms of breath and the relax step needed.

The most essential step toward experiencing the "TWIM" or aware jhānas is the correct practice of Right Effort; in particular, the *Tranquilize* step as defined in the suttas, or what we call the *Relax Step*. In Pāli, it is *passam bhayaṃ*. The relax step is the key to removing hindrances (and craving) through true Right Effort, which allows this different kind of jhāna to arise, an aware jhāna.

In both the Satipaṭṭhāna Sutta and Ānāpānasati Sutta it says: "As the student breathes in, he knows that he breathes in…when he breathes out, he knows that he breathes out." You don't focus on the breath alone but simply know that you are breathing. You simply *understand* that you are breathing.

The Pāli word for this is *sati,* which is to observe and to know. You know what a long breath is and you know what a short breath is. This just means to observe whatever is there in a light-minded way without trying to control it. You don't make a short breath long or a long breath short, you don't breathe in deeply or change the breath in any way and don't focus tightly on the breath — you just understand what is happening.

If someone said to you, "Do you know where you are?" you would look around and say, "Yes, I am in my garden." You don't focus and concentrate on the garden — you don't peer inside the bushes, look under rocks; you just know you are in the garden.

The Buddha makes this process even clearer with the next step where he says that "breathing in…and out he experiences the whole body." He's not saying to observe the breath. He's saying that as he breathes, he is experiencing the whole body. He is mindful of what is happening, both inside and outside. This softens the attention to encompass a greater field of awareness.

But then there comes the most important step in the Satipaṭṭhāna sutta's instruction, which is omitted or overlooked by other methods and practices. "The student *tranquilizes* the bodily formation on the in-breath…and he *tranquilizes* the bodily formation on the out-breath" [italics added]. This is the critical step that will lead you to the elimination of craving and the attainment of Nibbāna!

Why is this relax step ignored or just treated as a general "relax-the-body" step? Other methods don't value the importance of this. It isn't seen as an active step in practice — it is just understood as a general relaxing but not an active relaxing of tension in the head, a tension that is actually contained *in* the thought itself. In fact, it is a critically important step that runs counter to deep concentration, because focusing tightly creates tension, not tranquility.

What is it that you are relaxing? You are relaxing the tension and tightness which are signs of craving — craving that gives rise to thinking and to all kinds of habitual emotional tendencies, causing mind to wander away into daydreams and thoughts. What is all this? They are Mental Formations.

The Buddha addresses all this "noise" of the distractions and asks us to relax and tranquilize this also. Here is the quote from the Ānāpānasati Sutta MN 118. This *follows* the instruction to tranquilize the bodily formation.

> MN 118. *"He trains thus: 'I shall breathe in experiencing the mental formation'; he trains thus: 'I shall breathe out experiencing the mental formation. ' He trains thus: 'I shall breathe in tranquillizing the mental formation'; he trains thus: 'I shall breathe out tranquillizing the mental formation.'"*

So here we see the Buddha is asking us to specifically relax both the body and mind as a total process and specifically to relax the thoughts, which are the mental formations, that come up.

Why does the thinking come up? Everything draws your attention to it: thoughts, feelings, sensations, etc. Pleasant feelings are beckoning you to come and "taste" them and unpleasant feelings are poking you to dislike them because they are painful. It is how suffering is born. The mind is running free after this and that with no restraint. Gradually you come to see how this really is suffering!

Noticing distractions, or hindrances, arise and ignoring them or pushing them away, or following the advice to "clench your teeth and put your tongue up against the roof of your mouth…to remove them and to destroy them,"[1] is not the way to let go of distractions. Why? Because you haven't let go of the cause of that distraction, which is craving, the pulling of mind into thought.

Adding a step to actively relax into the tension and tightness in the head that pulls your mind away is what the Buddha found steadily reduces the energy of those distractions. The distraction will fade away naturally on its own because you've relaxed the tightness and tension feeding it. The more we pay attention to something the greater our attention is drawn and thoughts are created. Releasing your attention reduces thoughts and tension. We want to actively release our attention to distractions. We don't want to push them away — that just makes them stronger.

The Buddha called this Right Effort (*Sammā Vāyāma*). In TWIM it is called the 6Rs. This is the way hindrances are removed, and craving is eliminated bit by bit. We will discuss this process later as we go into the instructions.

In Majjhima Nikāya (MN) No. 36 the Mahāsaccaka Sutta it clearly states that after the Buddha tried to control his mind through "clenching his teeth" and so on, he found that his efforts, rather than getting control over his mind, led to the tiring out of his energy and brought on restlessness:

---

[1] *Majjhima Nikāya 20 Sec 2. This sutta is one that appears to have text from MN 36. However, in MN 36 it was shown how this advice was rejected by the Buddha.*

"[I] crushed mind with mind and sweat ran down from my arm-pits. But, although tireless energy was aroused in me and unremit-ting mindfulness was established, my body was overwrought and uncalm because I was exhausted by the painful striving."[iv]

This exertion did not work. Attempting to control the hindrances in this extreme way is just using aversion to push away what you don't want. There is no letting go here but only pushing away. We have created another hindrance. How many times have you heard some meditators say, "Darn it, I just can't make my mind do what I want it to do, it's really making me mad!" You can't use a hindrance to eliminate a hindrance! In other words, control will not work. Something else must be the correct path…

There is an article on the internet in which a jhāna meditation teacher wrote about his self-retreat practicing concentration meditation. He said he did a nine-month retreat and the first four months were spent "fighting" with his mind to stay on his breath! What? Fighting? How does that bring tranquility? Isn't there a faster way to get progress? Yes, there is! Hold on, did you just say four months to get concentrated?

Concentration practice tries to control mind and push away distracting thoughts and sensations. It both focuses down onto the object and then pushes away the wandering mind. The Buddha in the texts tells us not to suppress what he calls the defilements. In the Anguttara Nikāya, Samādhi Sutta in several places this is quite clear:

AN 5.27 …(4) The knowledge arises that is personally yours: 'This concentration is peaceful and sublime, gained by full tran-quilization, and attained to unification; it is not reined in and checked by forcefully suppressing the defilements.'

And notice the word above — Concentration in pāli is actually samādhi which Venerable Punnaji already has translated as Tranquil State of Wisdom or a state of collectedness. The above is the Samādhi Sutta, and it is named and translated as "Concentration, " and that is wrong. Are you beginning to see that the concentration methodology that the Buddha had already rejected keeps trying to make its way back into the teachings?

Since what you are trying to achieve is the removal of craving, you must see and understand it, not push it away. Absorption just puts it on the shelf such that when you come out of the absorption jhāna, the hindrances come back even stronger; like a vicious dog — you open the gate, now he attacks you with full force. Instead of pushing away the distraction, you simply relax into it and accept that it is there.

The Buddha found that relaxing the tension and tightness from the things that are pulling your mind away will gradually reduce the energy of those distractions. Finally, after relaxing enough of tension and tightness, the distraction will fade away on its own.

Why? It is because you are not feeding it. You are not reacting to it. This is what "tranquilizing" means: relaxing any tension or tightness that is whisking you away into thinking.

When you react to your wandering mind with aversion ("I don't like this!"), the reaction itself is the craving you are trying to remove. You need to *tranquilize* this reaction. Relax into it. Soften into it. Let it be. Let go of "beating yourself up."

As it occurs in the suttas, *tranquilize* is an action verb. It involves removing, by softening and purposely relaxing into, any tightness and tension in mind or body. It is not just a general relaxing of the mood or the body.

You see a beautiful woman walking down the street. Your mind has a pleasant feeling and craving arises, "I like her." You can feel your mind tightening around the form of the woman. Then comes thoughts about her, "Wow, I haven't seen her around before, wonder where she came from…" So, if we are sitting and we are using concentration meditation, and we start thinking over this experience of the lovely lady, we pull, or even jerk, our mind back to our object of meditation. We try to hold it there, pushing away this distraction.

But because we did not allow that distracting mind that arose to be there by itself, and actively relaxed the tension and tightness around it (sensual desire), we had even more, thoughts. We keep thinking more thoughts because the craving embedded in those thoughts keeps generating even more thinking.

Then we start getting upset because our thoughts are out of control and get frustrated and think what it would be like to constantly have lustful thoughts — constantly thinking and unable to be quiet. Then we think even more about it and get completely lost. A daydream could just turn into a nightmare!

The answer to this problem is the moment the image arose, and the pleasant feeling arose you would want to start relaxing into that perception right away. You want to release your attention from it, relax the tightness around it. Then the rest of the thoughts don't come up. You also don't get frustrated because you have truly let go and have not suppressed anything.

The word "tranquilize" in modern use often refers to stress relief. One might use a tranquilizer drug to take the stress away. In much the same way, we are tranquilizing the hindrance and taking away its tension and tightness.

Returning to The Buddha's Awakening story he sat in meditation again, but this time he relaxed and let go of the "tight mental fist" wrapped around those thoughts that pulled his mind out of the present. He relaxed into and tranquilized the tightness arising in his mind, in his head.

In the first watch of the night, the Buddha followed this method. He reached the fourth (Tranquil Aware) jhāna. When one adds the relax step, progress in the jhāna practice is indeed swift! The Buddha called progress "immediately effective" or *akāliko* in pāli.

From there the triple-knowledge arose: he remembered his past lives, experienced other realms, and realized how karma worked. At last, through seeing with wisdom (understanding dependent origination), he attained Nibbāna that very next morning.

Chapter Three: What is Jhāna?

The Buddha's process of awakening was what is called the "Three Knowledges" (*Tevijjā*). But the process of going through the jhānas is the same. More on this later.

What he taught the most, however, as in the Anupada Sutta which we are going to study next, is the path that goes through all the four material jhānas, the four immaterial states and on to Nibbāna. Again, these are the Tranquil Aware jhānas, not the absorption jhānas of yoga or other methods.

In the Majjhima Nikāya, the Buddha teaches jhānas in 50 suttas out of 152.[v] Clearly, the Buddha recommends the jhāna path to awakening; it just needs to be the *right type* of jhāna!

In addition to the fact that the tranquil aware (TWIM) jhānas will take you all the way to Nibbāna, a significant advantage with the aware jhānas is that they develop in a fraction of the time it takes to attain the absorption jhānas.

Consider that the Buddha taught many uneducated farmers as well as princes. He had to have a simple system of meditation that was "immediately effective" (*akāliko*). These farmers didn't have the time for, or interest in, a practice that took a long time to understand and master.

Relaxing tension and tightness eventually eliminate hindrances. With one-pointed concentration practice, all you are doing is suppressing hindrances for a short period of time. The same ones just keep coming back after your concentration power diminishes, so you must drive them away again each time you sit.

With the absorption jhānas, meditators dislike being disturbed from their meditation — for example, a loud sound arises, and dislike comes up. For the most part, the reaction to a hindrance is aversion or restlessness. You try to beat that hindrance away. In TWIM, you are "treating the illness" right there, removing the tension and tightness from the hindrance so that it loses its power.

Comparing Aware and Concentration Jhāna

As we sit in the *aware* jhānas, we can still hear sounds, and if the teacher calls us, we hear this and can respond right away. Someone might tap us on the shoulder and say something. We will feel it, and we can choose to respond or not. At the same time, when a loud motorcycle is outside the meditation hall, the mental balance is there — we hear it but pay no attention to it. Mind uses the relax step to observe, accept, and let go of the hindrance that pulls our attention away.

When you get into the higher aware jhānas, you do experience a sort of pulling away from the body because, in the immaterial *(arūpa)* jhānas, where there is only mind, it is operating on a subtler level — the senses have receded into the background. Only when there is *contact* do you notice the outside world. The word *contact* here means something happens to draw your attention — something unexpected like the teacher calling or the phone ringing.

Some teachers may advise you to stay away from (concentration) jhānas because you could become attached or even addicted to them. Actually, this *can* be true for absorption, one-pointed concentration jhānas, as they can become really intense. You might become caught by them because some are very blissful, and you could stop right there.

I have read accounts on discussion sites online where people experience absorption jhānas and think they are enlightened. They talk about how blissful it is yet they have only attained the first jhāna — there is still so much more to be learned!

But why would the Buddha give you a practice that had potential pitfalls like this? And wouldn't a student naturally want to move on and see what's next?

Based on the sutta texts the Buddha did not give us the absorption jhānas. He had already rejected them in the first part of his journey (sutta MN 36). You never need to worry about becoming attached to the aware jhānas. It's like saying you are attached to the third grade and never want to progress to the fourth because you don't want to learn anything new again.

With the aware jhānas, we are always looking to progress, to see what is next. In the suttas many times it is said that the meditator can easily experience this or that aware jhāna state, but that he knows this is not the *final* experience — that there is more to be done. So, the meditator keeps going. Progress does not stop.

In MN 105, Sunakkhatta Sutta, it says that the meditator, upon attainment of the realm of nothingness, now looks forward to the realm of neither-perception-nor-non-perception. He wants nothing to do with the previous state and, in fact, even considers it to be repulsive:

> 14. *"It is possible, Sunakkhatta, that some person here may be intent on the base of neither-perception-nor-non-perception. When a person is intent on the base of neither-perception-nor-non-perception, only talk concerning that interests him, and his thinking and pondering are in line with that, and he associates with that kind of person, and he finds satisfaction in that. But when talk about the base of nothingness is going on, he will not listen to it or give it ear or exert his mind to understand it. He does not associate with that kind of person, and he does not find satisfaction in that.*

> 15. *"Suppose a person has eaten some delicious food and thrown it up. What do you think, Sunakkhatta? Could that man have any desire to eat that food again?"*

> *"No, venerable sir. Why is that? Because that food is considered repulsive."*

The experiences you have when you practice an aware jhāna are unlikely ever to be repeated in the same way again. They are stages of progress. For example, when one gets an insight, it can unleash quite a bit of joy. But don't expect that again. You have now acquired that understanding, and there is no more to be learned from that insight. That one is "in the books."

Progress using the relax step is incredibly fast. In the Satipaṭṭhāna Sutta, the Buddha says awakening can happen in a single lifetime, in seven years, six years, five years…or even *as little as seven days*. When you follow the instructions precisely, your progress can be very quick.

On a typical ten-to-fourteen-day TWIM retreat, most students will get to the 4th jhāna, and many of those will get into the higher *arūpa* (formless) bases or jhānas. A few might even be successful *(the first experience of the awakening)*. It doesn't happen every retreat, but some people are just ready for it. They understand and follow the directions perfectly and have a successful retreat in every sense of the word!

When we release the tension and tightness from a hindrance, it gradually disappears. When that happens, you will have joy. For the first time, you have become free of craving until another hindrance shows up.

This experience is the basis for the *First* Tranquil Aware jhāna: a fully energetic, balanced, and sublime deep state of mind from which one can clearly see the impersonal processes of mind. From here you begin to see deeply into all twelve links of dependent origination, and in due time letting go of all conditions will come upon an unconditioned state!

In summary, TWIM   is not a *Concentration* meditation practice — it is a *Collected* meditation practice.

Chapter Four: Types of Concentration Practice

The Many Methods of Concentration Practice

I want to summarize the major types of concentration or absorption meditation techniques that exist in Buddhist practices today, especially in the Theravada tradition. This doesn't include all of them but the predominant generic types. They include the following:

- **Full Absorption** Concentration using meditation objects like the breath, visualizations, candle flames, or colored discs to become fully absorbed into the object.

- **Dry Insight** where the meditator does not become absorbed into the object but uses observation to develop insight — dry means without the use of deep one-pointed absorption concentration.

- **Concentration Insight Meditation** a mixture of the above using full absorption concentration to develop all eight absorption jhānas and then emerge and observe mind and develop insight.

We have already discussed Concentration-created Full Absorption meditation so let us look at the second point.

Dry Insight

Today, in Theravada, there are some different types of practices. There is one called straight Vipassanā (also called

"Dry Insight" or Insight Meditation) that was developed by Venerable Mahāsi Sayadaw of Burma. A similar system is the body awareness practice of sweeping developed by U Ba Khin of Burma now taught worldwide by S.N. Goenka of India. They avoid jhānic concentration-absorption. As discussed previously, students are told jhānas should be avoided as they might become attached to them as a distraction to their "real" work with the dry insight awareness exercise.

You are told that there is a shortcut around the *perceived* long, arduous development of jhānas by developing a technique of sweeping the body with awareness. By observing bodily sensations and seeing their true nature, you are told you will attain awakening.

In the "Dry Insight" Mahāsi tradition, you are told to follow the breath and make mental notes — "noting" — or making verbal, mental notes like "hearing, hearing," or "hot, hot" when your attention moves away from your breath or walking practice.

They say this will get you to Nibbāna very quickly, much faster than the use of the (absorption) jhānas that can take many months or years to achieve. Mahāsi Sayadaw says you can attain Nibbāna in, as little as, one thirty-day retreat with the "dry insight" method. This is why many people are attracted to this system for this claimed benefit. It appears to be fast and well laid out with clear instructions and stages of progress.

I remember reading this statement from a book by Admiral Shattuck about Vipassanā course in Burma forty years ago and getting very excited. I envisioned myself as this holy, enlightened person on the bus ride back from my first thirty-day retreat. Then I could take it easy…

Indeed, I did start retreating in a Denver basement that had been broken up into sections with drapes It was taught by a Sri Lankan trained American man who was extremely serious and demanded that we stay up until midnight and then wake up at 4am to start again. And that was my first retreat — thirty days — felt more like incarceration by the end of it. I was nineteen, forty-three years ago…

Chapter Four: Types of Concentration Practice

I tried that path for many years, experiencing most of the "Insight Knowledges" or ñāṇas that are said to indicate progress in that method. Later, I lived and worked at a Vipassanā center in San Jose, California, but the experiences I had with this method did not produce the personality change that the suttas indicate one should expect from meditation. Those insight experiences were very intense and happened just like Mahāsi Sayadaw wrote, but I was the same old neurotic self after the retreat. Perhaps I was a little kinder — or just deluded into thinking I was holier because of seeing these knowledges.

A 28-year-old Bhante Vimalaraṁsi, not yet a monk — he had a different "layman name" at that time — showed up at the center. Being a skilled carpenter and having built houses in San Francisco, he volunteered to build our meditation hall. It was a beautiful job with white carpets and stained glass.

I met him again years later in 2006, after a twenty-five-year gap. He had become a monk and gone to Burma, and had spent many years at the famous Mahāsi Meditation Center in Yangon. He trained under Venerable U Panditā Sayadaw and later with Venerable U Janaka practicing Mahāsi style Vipassanā.

I came to understand from Bhante that even in Burma (Myanmar), progress for the meditators was very difficult to achieve. He observed many students while he practiced there. He did many three-month retreats and, finally, a two-year retreat. It had taken all those retreats and experiences before he was told by his teacher that he had achieved the final result. That's a bit longer than thirty days! Later, he questioned this "attainment" because his experience didn't match with the suttas. Even after he had completed all those retreats, he did not feel like he experienced a fundamental personality change.

When I contacted him, he told me about his experiences in Burma in detailed emails. My confidence in his detailed descriptions of what he had attained in Vipassanā Insight practice reached a point where I realized that perhaps Vipassanā itself was the problem. It wasn't creating the change that one would expect. He had taken it to the limit and experienced all sixteen knowledges and now had decided to move on to something else.

When I looked at his website, it seemed very strange. He talked about smiling and relaxing — No motivational "have to push harder" talk. He said, "if you can't smile then laugh." What? He just wasn't "serious" enough! And this is serious practice, right?! Or is *that* the problem?

The "Dry Insight" practice or the Mahāsi Vipassanā method seems to me to be another form of concentration, a one-pointed and focused meditation practice. What is attained is accomplished by pushing away the hindrances and grasping hard onto the meditation object instead of simply "knowing" the object as the suttas say to do. It is a powerful, focused bearing down on the object, without the Relax step.

They say, "Go into your pain and get into the middle of it. See its nature of arising and passing away." Keep looking at it and noting it until it passes away — but that is controlling your awareness, which creates tension. Goenka teaches something similar with a sweeping exercise, but with the same type of mindfulness that focuses down on the sensations arising. The sweeping method does acknowledge distractions and lets them be and moves on, but it misses the whole relaxing step of removing the tension and tightness from the distraction. This technique is still a type of concentration practice, focusing on sensations rather than the breathing.

With the TWIM meditation, you observe a painful feeling, knowing it is there, you release your attention from it. You relax any tension and tightness that is bringing your awareness to the pain. Do not dwell on it; that is, don't think about it, analyze it, or bring aversion into it. That doesn't work. That doesn't relieve the tightness and tension.

By focusing down on that painful feeling — with an already tensed up mental state — and seeing it closer you will not gain further insight to release you from suffering — there is only more suffering. Bhante describes having done the Mahāsi process and finally getting beyond the pain, but it was just a temporary suppression of the pain. He said he had beaten it into submission during his meditation and finally, it had been forced away.

This type of meditation does, indeed, provide progress in the Vipassanā ñāṇas, which are stages of dry insight explained in the Visuddhi Magga. They are very real and thus provide much credibility to the practice. There are nine, twelve, or sixteen knowledges (depending on which text you read) that arise when following the instructions just like the Visuddhi Magga and Mahāsi's books say to do.

When we investigate, however, we find that these stages of insight are not in the suttas. When we practice with the relax step, they do not appear. Bhante explains that he did experience these insights and knowledges all the way to the knowledge of reviewing the path (the highest of the insight knowledges that arises after the attainment of Nibbāna), yet he was disappointed in the fact that he did not experience the personality change and awakened state he had expected.

I think people are impressed by this "dry insight" system because it does give the results it promises,[vi] and these results are very interesting. But so is an acid trip, which also can lead one to see impermanence, suffering, and impersonality if you have a Buddhist background and setting — but you will not see dependent origination.

The Buddha describes the seeing of the links of dependent origination as the door to Nibbāna. He says that one who sees the links will definitely see the three signs of impermanence, suffering, and non-self, but one who *only* sees the three signs will not automatically see dependent origination.

It is seeing and understanding dependent origination deeply that brings about personality change. This is why when you come out of the *absorption* meditative state versus the aware jhāna state, your personality, with all its neuroses, is still intact, is still the same. You only see things at a surface level because there is still craving there, just temporarily put aside. You have not seen at the deepest level revealing those most subtle of mental processes.

Many Vipassanā meditators find that their practice drops off after a certain point, and many will think that it is their own fault that they are not advancing. They think that they just need to do more retreats; they need to push even harder. Finally, many give up and think it was them and not the practice that was the problem. They think: "Maybe next lifetime I will be stronger. I'll have more merit!"

I had these experiences, and had no *real* change, and gave up practicing. I kept up with Buddhist studies, but lost interest in the practice and always wondered whether I had just missed something that everyone else had figured out!

Concentration Insight (vs. Dry Insight)

It is true that the absorption jhānas are very intense, and you could get attached to them. They completely push away the hindrances for a short period, and you come out of the jhānic state experiencing great bliss and happiness. But it doesn't last. Moreover, you don't learn anything from it. It is like a drug that you take, and later you just come down, and that's the end of that. It can be a kind of addiction, escaping into a bliss realm and getting away from life for a short period of time.

In another twist on concentration absorption practice you learn absorption jhāna practice, but then you are instructed that when you come out of that concentrated state, you are to observe with what is thought to be this "powerful mindfulness," after coming out of the absorption, the states that are arising and passing away at that very moment. You shine this powerful light on your arising mental states.

You are told to notice the foundations of mindfulness; notice the three signs inherent in them of impermanence, suffering, and impersonality. Teachers of this method claim that when you see these signs with the powerful awareness from the absorption jhāna experience you gain strong insights, and ultimately experience

Nibbāna. They use the suttas to back up this practice method, but they are misunderstanding the suttas.

The suttas explain the factors that make up the jhānas. They do talk about their impermanent and impersonal nature and how, by observing these factors of mind, you will gain insight — but not by suppressing craving and hindrances with absorption concentration. It is by allowing the hindrances to arise and gently release them or control them and they naturally fade away.

These concentration practices are all based on the Visuddhi Magga. Again, it says that once you attain the jhāna, you exit out of that jhāna and start to observe with the power of the concentration obtained. You use mindfulness to observe the mental processes. In this way, seeing how it works, you understand its nature of impermanence, suffering, and impersonality (anicca, dukkha, anattā). The Visuddhi Magga stresses that this insight is so profound that you attain Nibbāna.

Some claim that this is what the suttas mean when they talk about the meditator observing the factors and characteristics of the jhānas. They use the suttas to back up this technique when actually this isn't what was meant at all.

In the Anupada Sutta, it says the meditator observes many factors as they go through the jhānas. But they are already in the jhānas seeing these factors and don't need to *come out* to observe this. In fact, as soon as the jhāna disappears, so do the jhāna factors. They don't exist outside the jhāna. You can't observe them later.

The powerful, happy concentration jhāna state that the mind has just emerged from has suppressed all the craving that was causing the suffering in the first place. What was the craving that was being suppressed? It was the hindrances. What is the goal of meditation? Eliminating the hindrances and purifying the mind. In your practice, if we push the hindrances aside with strong concentration, how can we ever hope to understand them and their root cause?

The Concentration Insight meditator (using the absorption jhānas) will see the aggregates arising and passing away. He may, in fact, see some impermanence, suffering, and impersonality, but he won't see the links of dependent origination deeply.

Most people, who are reading the suttas, only know about the concentration-absorption practice. They are not aware of a tranquil aware jhāna. When Sāriputta says in the Anupada sutta that one is aware of the factors of the first jhāna as they occur, it is because he is in the first jhāna describing them as they are happening right then.

So far, I have read no claims of anyone who has attained awakening by practicing this method of going into the absorption jhānas and then coming out and reviewing the mental factors. Many have described this practice, but none I have ever read declare that there are meditators who have been successful with it.

In the end, you can gain some understanding by observing mind, but you just can't get deep enough to see the links of dependent origination, and you certainly can't attain insight by analyzing or thinking about what you are observing.

Profound insight is beyond thought. There can be no craving left to obscure your vision which concentration meditation still contains. Seeing directly into mind with the absence of craving of the *aware* jhāna will lead to Nibbāna.

Caution with Absorption Concentration

One final word about concentration meditation: one-pointed concentration can be dangerous. That may be too strong a word, but yes, it is true. Ruth Denison, a famous meditation teacher in California, tried a Zen retreat as her first step toward investigating meditation as a path to enlightenment. Doing the breath meditation in a concentrated way she experienced a mental breakdown, and she ended up in a hospital.[2] After this, she rejected this method and

---

[2] *Dancing in the Dharma: The Life and Teachings of Ruth Denison, Sandy Boucher, 2006*

moved to a style of a more balanced awareness integrated with dance and movement that she developed on her own.

There have been many other concentration-caused breakdowns — just search the web for "concentration meditation danger, " and you will find any number of articles.

It is a little-known fact that after her own negative experience, Ruth worked at her center in Joshua Tree, California (Dhamma Dena Vipassanā Center), with people who had lost touch with reality because of absorption or dry insight practice. The connection of their mind to their body, to various degrees, had been disrupted. She worked with them to get their hands in the dirt, had them build stone monuments, and otherwise tried to bring back the connection to their bodies. These were people who came from traditions using concentration meditation as their practice. I was on several TWIM retreats at her center, and while there I heard Ruth talk about this issue.

On one retreat I was introduced to a person who had been sent there. She looked pretty miserable. She was withdrawn and had low energy and no ability to sit. There was a kind of hopelessness in her voice when she said hello. Ruth had a lot of luck bringing people back to balance, and I certainly hope she was successful with her.

In Vipassanā, especially, many people now talk about the "Dark Night of the Soul" stage in the meditation. This is a pretty new term for me, but it is simply talking about the higher stages of the meditation where the knowledge of fear arises, among other states.

These are standard levels of knowledge, and I went through them and was told just to ride it out. It never had a name like this, but I do know what it is. It is the fear of dying because you see that there is no Self there, however you have no balance, and the craving mind arises and comes in the form of great fear because you are taking all this personally.

There is nothing unpleasant like this that ever happens in TWIM meditation, if there is then you 6R or release and relax into it as just another hindrance. TWIM is the letting go of the craving mind and thus gaining more and more balance and happy states.

Mental breakdowns don't happen often, but it can happen when the meditator pushes too hard, striving to crush their hindrances with mental power rather than relaxing into them and letting them be. Meditation teachers who are using concentration jhānas point to the suttas for the verification that what they are doing is correct, but again they forget that the Buddha rejected those concentration methods.

In one popular practice of concentration jhānas, the author of a book on the concentration jhānas and their development states that "three out of a thousand students will experience the joy or *pīti* being turned on and then unable to be turned off… This is when the *pīti* gets stuck on and never seems to go away. This can last for weeks, months, even up to a year. Thankfully, this is quite rare since there aren't any really effective solutions other than waiting the thing out. What does seem to help is getting grounded — exercise, manual labor, and eating heavy foods, like meat…"[vii] He describes when *pīti* is left on it is like a high-energy, buzzing, unpleasant feeling that continues whether you are sitting or not. Sometimes it just only creates insomnia.

Another problem, that is also reported in the book, is sometimes students want to bypass the first jhāna intentionally because "…the intense *pīti* brings up painful memories."[viii] And there are issues with the second and third jhāna states where one is advised to bypass or do something to avoid a certain problem.

The suttas do not support the concentration-absorption jhānas or the dry insight method at all. They don't support the arising of painful states in a practice that is gradually eliminating craving step by step. Proponents say it's faster. So, are we saying the Buddha gave us the slow way?? The Buddha's supreme knowledge would have seen the best and fastest way. I think we can assume this.

Suttas Support TWIM

When the relax step is used, there are no negative states that arise. The suttas say you continue with your meditation, through the jhānas, and after the base of neither-perception-nor-non-perception, you keep meditating to what some call a ninth jhāna. This is the cessation of mind's movement completely.

Gradually the mental movement gets slower and slower starting at the 1st jhāna going to the base of neither-perception-nor-non-perception. There are eight steps or levels, and there is the point where mind finally just stops.

If you think about this, you are not going higher and higher in the meditation; you are going "lower and slower" until everything just stops.

There is no stopping progress in the meditation; it naturally moves along, and insights arise as they will until mind stops and enters cessation.

The basis and meditation object for Tranquil Wisdom Insight Meditation is Mettā and the four Brahmavihāras right from the suttas. There are some added methods used in TWIM like "breaking down the barriers" and sending mettā to a Spiritual Friend, which are very helpful in the beginning stages of the meditation. When your TWIM meditation has developed to a certain level, it then switches to and follows the suttas precisely, using the *pervading to the six directions* as taught in the Brahmavihāra method.

One thing that isn't used with this mettā practice and TWIM, which is used by the majority of other teachers, is repeating the same four statements over and over. This is a traditional way of developing Mettā meditation. With the TWIM method, you bring up the sincere feeling of the wish for loving-kindness and put that feeling in your heart. You surround your spiritual friend (your meditation object) with that feeling and suffuse him or her with that feeling.

The way most people are teaching mettā is an intellectual exercise instead of a feeling meditation by saying the same statements over and over again, which turns it into a mantra or a one-pointed concentration. Instead of making the wish over and over to be happy, in TWIM you use the wish to remind yourself to bring up the feeling of loving-kindness. Later, as your practice goes deeper you will drop the phrases entirely. The result of doing this is not a dry intellectual experience, but rather, a feeling exercise which uplifts mind and helps you to become happy.

Continually repeating the same statements allows no room for the feeling to develop — you must develop a sincere feeling and wish for your spiritual friend to be happy so the Mettā or loving-kindness can take hold. Rather than repeating the wishes, Bhante advises bringing up a smile to remind yourself of the feeling — a smile in your heart, in your mind and also on your lips.

Secular Buddhism

A new variation of Buddhism has taken hold called *secular* Buddhism. It teaches only the parts of Buddhism that we can see for ourselves and we do not need to believe in. For example, past lives are not considered part of the Buddha's teaching in secular Buddhism. We don't tend to see them and recall them for ourselves, here and now, (however, there are indeed, some students who recall past lives, and an entire industry of Past-Life Regression Hypnotherapists have sprung up to address past lives and psychological problems from these lives that have seeped into the present.)

It does seem like the purest secular Buddhist practice attempts to remove the *Buddha* from Buddhism. It offers a distorted view of Mindfulness as only a tool with which to therapeutically approach De-stressing and healing the individual. What happened to Nibbāna? What happened to profound insight into Impermanence and Impersonality? Where is Craving?

Chapter Four: Types of Concentration Practice

Secular Buddhism removes Buddhist concepts because they are seen as weird and are religious mumbo-jumbo and unnecessary to solving one's problems. There is even a magazine about *Mindfulness*, with that very title, which has not a single reference to the Buddha in it. All Pāli terms are left out.

I walked through the bookstore the other day, and Buddhism has been reduced to just one shelf now. Mindfulness books have gone over to Self-Help, leaving the Dali Lama alone with Thich Nhat Hahn to keep him company in the Eastern Religions section.

There is no mention of higher understanding or enlightenment. Mindfulness is just another tool that has been added to the psychotherapeutic toolkit. This is the watering down of Buddhism.

MBSR or Mindfulness-Based Stress Reduction is a program in which mindfulness is employed for the purpose of therapy. Buddhist ideas of impersonality and impermanence really don't play a major part. Dependent Origination is surely missing. It basically is about watching the breath and doing slow walking meditation to calm down the mind. The perceived goal is to reduce stress and anxiety. It is seen as not being possible to attain enlightenment and to permanently eliminate craving.

There are now even apps for your phone to give you a short five to ten minute guided breathing or body awareness meditation that you can do each day to de-stress. Intense mindfulness practice has been diluted since the beginning of the introduction of Buddhist meditation styles of Vipassanā and Goenka practice in the early 70's. There are *more* people meditating, however, now, less are going deeply into their practice.

Another blend of Buddhism is a meditation style called Advaita and is based on thousands year old Vedanta practices. It is a Hindu-based "non-dual" or a "philosophy of oneness" practice. Famous proponents of this are Eckart Tolle and Adyashanti. The practice focuses on observing whatever arises in the present moment and not trying to control or analyze. Some call this choiceless awareness. Just allowing what is there and letting mind calm and go deeper and following it down to a level of "Oneness." Tibetan Dzogchen practice is similar, in that it observes this open field of awareness without controlling the experience.

This practice can be quite useful to a point and is quite close to what the Buddha taught in being genuinely mindful. It certainly turns your practice to observing, rather than "trying" too hard to achieve a certain state or experience. You simply allow what is there, even to the point of inquiring "who is meditating" and "what are you trying to achieve?" This is the first step of letting go of the "controller." Adyashanti explains that instead of controlling the meditation, you *"let go* of the meditator!"

As one gets deeper and mind's activity slows, proponents explain that you will eventually see the underlying "essence" or "spirit" referred to by Tolle as "the Sacred." Adyashanti calls it coming to a state of "oneness;" unchanging and blissful. This is a variation of the belief in a soul or Higher Self. Unchanging meaning a permanent state.

At the end of the Brahmavihāra TWIM practice that is described here, the feeling of equanimity disappears. The meditator is now told to take this *quiet mind* as the object of their meditation. Observe any movements and release and relax those movements as they arise. Come back to the quiet mind.

This does sound like what the Vedanta practice or choiceless awareness achieves, and these meditation practices can be useful. However, they can't get beyond just a quiet mind to see below that. Since the relax step, the foundation of TWIM, is not employed here, you won't understand how to relax the mental tightness to go even deeper. With that tool, you go past the level where one might think that a permanent type of spirit resides, down to an even deeper level and ultimately the very nethermost – the beginning of mentality itself.

When your mind is just barely moving, and you are able to observe with powerful mindfulness, you won't be able to find such a thing as a self — only moments of consciousness arising and passing away, in a never-ending stream. From this insight arises, disenchantment, and then dispassion leading to awakening out of this dream of self.

Chapter Five: Beginning Practice

Now let us see how the TWIM meditation practice can take us through the four tranquil aware jhānas including the four formless bases contained in the fourth jhāna, culminating with the attainment of Nibbāna. If you follow what the suttas say without any added interpretation, then this is what will happen. This is the progress of Tranquil Aware Insight Meditation or TWIM.

The jhānas described from here on are the *tranquil aware* jhānas. In this type of jhāna, you are aware of both mind and body. The Buddha said we cannot ever understand ourselves unless we look at the totality of who we are and see the impersonal nature of everything that arises. We can't control anything by pushing it away or trying to stop what comes up. Only through acceptance of what is in the present, not fighting or controlling it, seeing it clearly without mental noise or craving, can we achieve release.

A word here about morality. The Buddha's system is built on a moral view of the world. If you do unwholesome actions, then painful results and mental states like hindrances follow. Do wholesome and wholesome follows. Meditation is completely wholesome. If you wish to be successful in your meditation, you should be following the five precepts as a minimum to achieve the best progress.

What are they? Not killing, not stealing, not lying or cursing, not being involved in sexual misconduct like adultery and not taking intoxicants or alcohol. It isn't hard, and it said that following these simple guidelines brings you a prosperous and happy existence in this life and the next.

Following these five precepts, prescribed by the Buddha as your moral baseline, will help your meditation to go very deep. By not committing any further harmful acts you will become free of guilt and remorse, and your mind will be peaceful and tranquil. For retreats, there are an additional three precepts to help you fine tune, including not eating after noon, not engaging in entertainment and not using perfumes or makeup.

Summary of the *Meditation* Instructions

The beginning meditator will spend a few days or weeks cultivating loving-kindness toward themselves and a "Spiritual Friend" by using phrases to help bring up the feeling of loving-kindness: "May I be happy," "May I be peaceful," "As I am happy I wish you to be happy." This process will take them to the 4th jhāna. As they progress they will move on to radiating mettā to the six directions and progress from the 4th jhāna to the base of nothingness and beyond.

Beginning Posture

Before meditating, it is helpful to find a relatively quiet place and to sit comfortably and upright.

Sitting cross-legged is not required, the full lotus is certainly not necessary. A sitting posture that is familiar to your body will be less distracting and more helpful than one in which you are uncomfortable or in pain. In the West, many meditators find sitting on the floor difficult. In that case, use a chair rather than causing yourself undue pain and discomfort. There is no "magic" in the floor.

Avoid leaning heavily back into the chair. Sit with your vertebrae stacked one on top of the other. The posture should be comfortable. The goals are to reduce any real physical cause of tension and pain and to improve alertness. We will have enough *mental* obstacles to keep us busy!

Beginning Lovingkindness Instructions

When you practice the *Mindfulness of Lovingkindness* meditation, begin by radiating loving and kind feelings to yourself. Remember a time when you were happy. When that happy feeling arises, it is a warm, glowing feeling.

Some of you may complain—we actually do hear this a lot—that you cannot recall any good memories. So then we ask, "Can you imagine holding a baby and looking into its eyes? Do you feel a loving feeling? When that baby smiles, do *you*?"

Another idea is to imagine holding a cute little puppy. When you look at the puppy, you naturally want to smile and play with him. The feeling you are creating is a warm, glowing, and sincere feeling radiating from your eyes, your mind, and your heart.

Once you have established this feeling, use this feeling to wish yourself happiness. "Just as I was happy then, may I be happy now." Continue with phrases like "May I be peaceful," "May I be happy," "May I be calm."

Do you know what it feels like to be peaceful and calm? Then *put that feeling* and *yourself* in the center of your heart and surround yourself with that happy feeling.

When that feeling fades, bring up another phrase to remind you of the feeling. "May I be tranquil," "May I be content," "May I be full of joy." Now give yourself a big "heart hug." Really and sincerely, wish yourself to be happy! Love yourself and mean it. This feeling is your object of meditation.

Each time the feeling fades, repeat the wish verbally a few times in your mind. Just repeat it enough times to bring up the feeling—*do not* make it a mantra! Saying a phrase over and over will not bring up the feeling we want — the phrase just reminds us to bring the feeling up. When the feeling comes up we drop the phrase.

There are a number of other teachers who focus on just saying the phrases over and over, and that doesn't work. That will just turn it into a concentration practice on the phrase.

Some people visualize easily; others do not. It is not important that you clearly *see* your object of meditation. Just *know* it is there. Keep the feeling of yourself in the center of your chest, wrapped in this happy and content feeling.

And, we do mean really *feel good!* Feel peaceful, or calm, or loving, or gentle, or kind, or giving, or joyful, or clear, or tranquil, or accepting. Be okay sitting and feeling this. It's *okay* to feel good, let yourself be there in the present, just feeling this contentment.

You have nowhere to go; you are on a little vacation from life now. There is nothing to do other than to be happy and radiate that feeling to yourself. Can you do that? Don't *try* to be happy. *Be* happy! Be content. Be at peace—right here, right now. You have our permission to be happy for at least the next thirty minutes!

This is a feeling meditation, but don't over observe the center of your chest trying to bring up a feeling of Lovingkindness. Don't force a feeling where there isn't one. Don't put the cart before the horse. Smile and feel that smile all through your body. As you say the phrases, bring this feeling up, and it will resonate in your heart area on its own. *Sincerely* wish yourself happiness. Believe it, and know that you *do* wish happiness for yourself. Just be with this feeling, know it is there, and smile with it.

There may be some blocks that come up such as saying to yourself, "No, I don't deserve to be happy like this!" This aversion to your own happiness is a distraction. Distractions will be covered shortly. We will explain the method to deal with them so that you can allow and train yourself to feel real Lovingkindness for a longer period of time.

Later, when you begin feeling this feeling toward others, know that similar blocks may come up and that these are distractions too. There is no reason that others should not be happy as well. The goal is to first accept and allow yourself to be happy and peaceful. It's okay. Then, since you feel that happiness in your own mind you will be happy to share that feeling with other beings.

When you sit, please don't move. Don't wiggle your toes; don't twitch or itch; don't rub; don't scratch; don't rock back and forth. Don't change your posture at all. Sit as still as the monk below. When you sit still the mind calms down. If there is any movement at all the mind will be distracted — just as jello sets up, it must be cooled and not jiggled around to solidify.

Smiling

This is a smiling meditation. The reason that you should smile is because it has been found that when the corners of your mouth go up, so does your mental state. When the corners of your mouth go down, so does your mental state.

Put a little smile on your lips, but don't stop there. Put a smile in your eyes even though your eyes are closed. You'll notice there can be a lot of tension in the eyes. Put a smile in your mind. And, especially, put a smile in your heart.

It can be a mechanical smile at first—eventually, it will turn into a sincere happy feeling. It should be a smile that conveys Lovingkindness. It's important to believe it! Smile with your lips, smile from your mind, and smile from your heart!

If your mind wanders away twenty-five times in a sitting, and twenty-five times you recognize it, release it, relax, re-smile, and return to your meditation, then you've had a good meditation. It definitely might not be a quiet and calm meditation, but it *is an active* meditation, and that can still be a *good* meditation!

Every time your mind wanders away and comes back, and you relax and smile, you are developing your ability to see a distraction and let it go. You are improving your Mindfulness, your observation power. As you practice, you will get better at it, and your powers of observation will get stronger.

Distractions

While you practice Mettā meditation in this way, your mind is going to wander. What do we mean by wander? You are with your object of meditation, which is the warm glowing feeling in the center of your chest. You are experiencing this feeling; then you are distracted by some thought or sensation. It might be a sensation of itching, a desire to cough, a burning sensation, or a painful feeling in your leg. It might be a memory of a conversation with a friend or of a trip to the lake. Or it could be a thought about something you need from the store.

Suddenly you are with that distraction rather than with your object of meditation. In other words, your attention is somewhere else. You are not sure how you got there or what you are supposed to be doing. Then you *remember* that you are meditating and that you are supposed to be on your object of meditation. *Remember*—that is the first part of the definition of mindfulness.

If you let go of your thinking about the distraction and relax slightly, you can observe that there is a tight mental fist wrapped around that sensation or thought. You can also observe that you don't want it there. You want it to go away. But, the more you want it to go away, the bigger and more intense the distraction becomes.

So your mind is on this itch, this pain, this thought. How did it get there? It didn't just jump there. There is a process that happens, and you begin to see how your mind moves from one thing to another. Don't *think* about that, but *observe* carefully how the process happens. We aren't talking here about analyzing why anything happens — simply *observe* what is happening. *Observe* the way the *mind moves and reacts* in the present — that is the second part of mindfulness.

The truth is that when a sensation is there, it's there! It's okay for it to be there. You are going to have distracting thoughts and sensations come up, and that's okay. Thoughts are not your enemy. In fact, they are opportunities.

Every thought, every feeling, every sensation that arises and distracts your mind also causes tightness.

The First Noble Truth is that there is suffering. The Second Noble Truth is that suffering is caused by Craving. The Third Noble Truth is that there is the cessation of suffering. The Fourth Noble Truth is that there is the path to the cessation of suffering. This path is the Eightfold Path.

This tightness is how you can recognize the very start of Craving and, as you may know, the Second Noble Truth says that craving is the cause of suffering! Life is not suffering; craving is what makes it so.

Distractions are telling you what you crave — the things to which you are attached. Seeing and understanding what you like and dislike is the first step toward letting go of those attachments.

Your brain has two lobes that are contained in three membranes called the *meninges*. It is like a bag wrapped around your brain and spine. Any time that there is a distraction, there is a perceptible movement in the brain, a tension or tightness, and the brain *seems* (some will disagree with this, but something *is* felt) to start to expand against this membrane. The thought causes this tightness or tension to arise, which we are actually able to observe for ourselves.

Any time you notice this tension and tightness, you want to actively relax and soften into it. By relaxing, you are releasing the Craving. More on this when we get to the 6Rs.

When Craving is released, there is a slight feeling of expansion in your head. Right after you relax, you will notice that your mind is very peaceful and calm. Your mind is alert, and there are no thoughts. At this time, you have a pure mind. Now bring that pure mind back to your object of meditation—the feeling of Lovingkindness and smiling—that warm, radiating, happy feeling. Now make another wish for your happiness, put that feeling into your heart, and radiate that happy feeling to yourself.

It does not matter how many times your attention is pulled away by a distraction. Thoughts and sensations don't go away the first time you notice them, and that's okay. As these distractions come back again and again, you will become increasingly familiar with how they arise. With practice, their intensity and frequency will subside.

Hindrances

The Buddha talked about five hindrances to meditation. Hindrances are distractions that will pull you away from your object of meditation—five troublemakers who will surely come calling!

Every distraction is based on at least one of the five hindrances. Often they come two or three at a time and gang up.

The Five Hindrances are:

1. Sensual Desire: "I like that," otherwise known as Lustful or Greedy Mind. You will hang onto things that are *pleasant* and want more. This will cause attachment to pleasant states of mind that have arisen in the past, and desire for pleasant states to arise in the future.

2. Anger, Aversion, Fear: "I don't like that." You will want to push away states of mind that you don't like. Or, you might experience fear or anger over *unpleasant* or painful feelings that have already arisen. You will try to push away and *control* anything causing you pain. You will even try to force your mind to experience things in a certain way that you think is *right* when you actually should just observe what is there. Now, that is really overly controlling!

3. Sloth and Torpor: Dullness and Sleepiness. These will cause lack of effort and determination because you've lost interest in your object of meditation. You will experience a mental fog. When you look at it closely, you actually see that it has tightness and tension in it. There is even Craving in sleepiness.

4. Restlessness: With Restlessness you constantly want to move and change, to do something other than what you are doing, to be somewhere other than here. Restlessness can manifest as very tight, unpleasant feelings in the body and mind.

5. Doubt: You are not sure you are following the instructions correctly, or even if this is the right practice. It makes you feel unsure of yourself and may even manifest as a lack of confidence in the Buddha's teaching or your teacher or both.

When the hindrances arise, your job is neither to like them nor to fight with them. Your job is to accept them, to *invite them in*, and to *"offer them tea"*!

Don't feed them with your attention. Forcing and not liking their being there just gives them the attention they crave and makes them stronger.

That's what happens with one-pointed concentration meditation. You force the hindrances away by practicing intense concentration.

However, as soon as you stop meditating they come back, sometimes even stronger.

If you just let hindrances be there, turning your attention to something that is wholesome instead, the energy inherent in them will gradually fade away. They will disappear like a fire that runs out of fuel. That's how you overcome the hindrances for good. The fire just goes out. In Pāli, Nibbāna translates as *"Ni"* or *no*, and *"bāna"* or *fire*. No Fire. No Craving. No hindrance.

The 6Rs

Now we are going to give you specific instructions on how to work with the hindrances in the way the Buddha taught.

Imagine, for a moment, the Bodhisattva resting under the Rose Apple tree as a young boy. He was not serious or tense; he was having fun, watching his father's festival. Right then he "attained to a pleasant abiding" (*jhāna*) as stated in the suttas. With a light mind, he was able to come to a very tranquil and aware state.

Later, on the eve of his enlightenment, after he had tried every method of meditation and bodily exercise that was known in India at that time, he remembered this state. And he realized that this simple state—this tranquil, aware, and happy state—was the key to attaining awakening. But how to convey this?

When he was teaching, the Buddha worked largely with uneducated farmers and merchants. He had to have a simple, effective practice that was easy and worked quickly. He had to have a method by which everyone could experience the path and benefits for themselves easily and immediately. This is how he was able to affect so many people during his lifetime.

Do you want to see clearly? It's easy! Lighten up, have fun exploring — relax, and smile! Relaxing and smiling leads you to a happier, more interesting practice.

That sounds like great advice, but how do you do it? When you have been carried away by distraction, and you lose your smile, just follow these steps:

1. *Recognize* that mind's attention has drifted away and that you are lost in thought. You have forgotten what you were doing. You are no longer on your object of meditation.

2. *Release* your attachment to the thought or sensation by letting the distraction be—by not giving it any more attention. Just stop feeding it. Just back away from it.

3. *Relax* any remaining tension or tightness caused by that distraction.

4. *Re-smile*. Put that smile back on your lips and in your heart. Feel that happy feeling of Lovingkindness again.

5. *Return* or redirect. Gently redirect mind's attention back to the object of meditation, that is, to Mettā. Continue with a gentle, collected mind to stay with your object of meditation.

6. *Repeat* this entire practice cycle. Repeat this practice whenever your attention is distracted away from your object of meditation.

We call these the "6Rs." They are drawn directly from the sutta text as part of Right Effort. The first four 'R's are the four right efforts, with the last two 'R's to remind you to Return and Repeat as needed.

Recognize

Repeat

Release

Return

Relax

Re-Smile

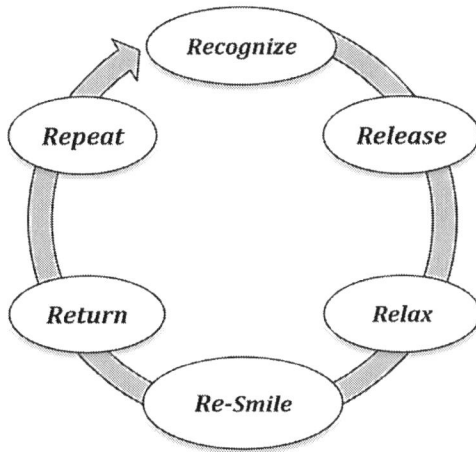

Notice that you never *push* anything away. You never try to control anything—trying to control is using Craving to eliminate Craving!

Please don't do the 6Rs for some slight noise in the background or a minor bodily feeling. As long as you are still with your feeling of Lovingkindness, just stay with that feeling and let it deepen. Ignore those slight distractions in the background. As a beginner do the 6Rs only if your attention is completely "gone" from the object.

In the explanation of the Eightfold Path in the suttas, one of the components is Right Effort. Right Effort and the 6Rs are exactly the same things.

What is Right Effort?

1. You notice that an unwholesome state has arisen.

2. You stop paying attention to that unwholesome feeling, letting it be there by itself with no pushing away or holding on to it.

3. You bring up a wholesome feeling.

4. You stay with that wholesome feeling.

The 6Rs just add the *Return* and *Repeat* to complete the cycle. We are practicing Right Effort by repeating the 6Rs cycle again and again. We see and experience for ourselves what suffering is and how to relieve it.

You notice what causes you to become tense and tight, and then how to reach its cessation by releasing and relaxing and bringing up a wholesome object. You discover how to exercise the direct path to the cessation of suffering. This happens each time you *Recognize* and *Release* an arising feeling, *Relax,* and *Re-smile*. Notice the Relief.

When you look at the benefits discussed in the sutta about the Dhamma, there is a phrase that says the Dhamma is "*immediately effective.*" By practicing the 6Rs, you fulfill this statement! When you relax the tension or tightness caused by a distraction, you immediately experience the Third Noble Truth, the *cessation* of suffering.

In other words, you are purifying the mind by relaxing and letting go of suffering. You see this for yourself.

Then you bring up a wholesome object by *smiling* and return mind's attention back to Mettā, which is a wholesome feeling.

You do not have to practice for long periods—months or years—to feel relief. You can see it right after the Relax step of the 6Rs. You notice the moment of a pure mind, free from Craving.

By repeating the 6Rs over and over, depriving the hindrances of attention, their fuel, you will eventually replace all of the unwholesome mental habits with wholesome ones. In this way, you bring up only wholesome states and will eventually achieve the cessation of suffering.

To be successful in meditation, you need to develop your mindfulness skill and observation power. Also, keeping up your sense of fun and exploration is important. This helps to improve your mindfulness. The 6Rs training develops these necessary skills.

Sometimes people say this practice is simpler than they thought. Some have actually complained to the teacher because they want this meditation to be more complicated!

Now let us go through each of the steps in more depth.

Recognize

Mindfulness remembers to observe and recognize movements of mind's attention from one thing to another—that is, from the meditation object to the distraction. This observing notices any movement of mind's attention away from the object of meditation. One can notice a slight tightness or tension as mind's attention begins to move toward the arising phenomenon.

Pleasant or painful feelings can occur at any one of the six sense doors. Any sight, sound, odor, taste, touch or thought can cause a distraction to arise. With careful nonjudgmental observation, you will notice a slight tightening sensation arising both in mind and physically in the brain itself.

Recognizing early movement of mind is vital to successful meditation. You then continue on to…

Release

When a thought about something arises, release it. Let it be there without giving any more attention to it. The content of the distraction is not important at all, but the mechanics of *how* it arose are important! Don't analyze it or try to figure out why it is there; let it be without keeping mind's attention on it. Without your mind's attention, the distraction loses energy and passes away. When you do not keep your attention on it, a distraction and the mental chatter about it ceases. Mindfulness then reminds the meditator to…

Relax

After releasing the thought and allowing it to be by itself without trying to watch it or get involved in it, there is a subtle, barely noticeable tightness or tension remaining within mind and body.

To remove this remaining tension, the Buddha introduced a *relax* step. The suttas[3] call the relax step *"tranquilizing* the bodily formation." This is true especially in your head, which is part of your body.

It means to "unclench" your attention from and around the thought. It is more than just letting it go. It actively softens and relaxes, and lets the distraction be there, which then weakens its power. Gradually it disappears completely on its own.

Please do not skip this step! It is the *most important* part of this meditation. It is the *missing step* we talked about in the introduction. It is the key to progress!

Without performing this step of relaxing every time you are distracted from your meditation object, you will not experience the close-up view of the cessation of the tightness caused by Craving. You will not feel the relief as this tension is relaxed.

Remember that Craving always manifests first as a tightness or tension in both your mind and body. The *Relax* step gives you a kind of "Mundane Nibbāna." You have a momentary opportunity to see and experience the true nature of and relief from tightness and suffering while performing the *Release* and *Relax* steps. Mindfulness then continues to remember to…

Re-Smile

If you have listened to the Dhamma talks on our website, you might remember hearing about how smiling is an important aspect of the meditation. Learning to smile and raising the corners of the mouth slightly helps the mind to be observant, alert, agile, and bright. Getting serious, tensing up, or frowning causes mind to become heavy and your mindfulness to become dull and slow. Insights

---

3   This Relax step is found in all suttas where the Buddha gives meditation instructions. The Pāli word for tranquilize is *passambhaya.* See for example the Majjhima Nikāya, suttas 10:5 or 118.

become more difficult to see, thus slowing down your understanding of Dhamma.

Return

Redirect your mind back to your object of meditation. Gently redirect the mind and don't "jerk" it back before you are ready. Make this a harmonious movement, a movement that is timely and not forced.

Repeat

Repeat this entire practice cycle as often as needed. Stay with your object until you slip, and then run the 6Rs again.

Spiritual Friend

For the first ten minutes of your sitting, radiate Lovingkindness to yourself. Wrap yourself up in that happy, tranquil feeling using the previous instructions. For the rest of the sitting, radiate loving and kind thoughts to a Spiritual Friend. What is a Spiritual Friend?

Now we will select our next object of meditation, the Spiritual Friend. It is very important that they are a living person, of the same sex, and are not a member of your family.

When the Spiritual Friend is of a different sex, it may lead to lustful feeling, and this complicates your experience. This is the traditional way of teaching Mettā. If this instruction does not fit you, then just make sure the person you select does not raise lustful feelings in your mind when you are radiating loving-kindness— remember, you will be spending a long time with this person.

Your Spiritual Friend should be someone who you deeply respect and sincerely wish well. They are someone who makes you smile when you think of them. It might be a favorite teacher or counselor who has your highest goals in mind. It might be a friend who always has your back and supports whatever you do.

Please do not use a member of your family as your Spiritual Friend, because family members are too close to you. Family members will be brought into your practice at a later time, but for now, they may raise hidden issues that interfere with the practice. Initially, we want to keep this easy and uncomplicated. Do not radiate to a person who is dead—the feeling will not arise correctly, as there is no personal connection that can be made.

You make the wish for your spiritual friend in this way: "As I feel this happiness in myself, may you be happy and peaceful!" Wrap them up in the feeling of Lovingkindness, place them in the center of your heart, and smile at them as you are doing this. Really be *sincere* about this. Really believe it. The more you believe it, the stronger the feeling will become.

Continue wishing them well and see them in your mind's eye, but don't put too much emphasis on the actual mental image of them. Again, some people are very good at visualizing, and some are not. Just know who they are and that you wish them well.

The phrases are a way of priming the pump—they evoke the feeling. As you make that wish, shift your attention to the feeling itself. Remember that your object of meditation is the *feeling*. Stay with that feeling and let it grow as it will. Don't force it; just give it some gentle encouragement.

Sooner or later the feeling will fade. When it does, repeat the phrases again. It is not helpful to repeat phrases rapidly. That makes the phrase feel mechanical. Rather, say it sincerely and rest for a few moments with the feeling it evokes. Repeat a phrase again only if it hasn't brought up the feeling.

Some people ask, "Are we 'sending' this feeling outward to the Friend?" No, we are not sending anything. We are just seeing our Friend in the center of our heart and wishing for him or her to be happy. We are not sending, telegraphing, or "overnighting" any sort of feeling. When a candle radiates warmth and light, is it actively sending that feeling out? No, it radiates out because that is the nature of warmth and light. In the same way, we surround and immerse our Friend with this feeling, wishing it for them, and seeing them smiling and happy.

This process is a combination of three things arising: the radiating feeling in your heart, the mental phrase, and your image of yourself or your spiritual friend. About 75 percent of your attention should be on the radiating of the feeling, 20 percent on feeling the wish, and just a little, say 5 percent, on visualizing your spiritual friend.

Some people think they should make the visualization a bigger part of their practice. Then they complain about having tightness in their head. This is because they are pushing the idea of seeing their Spiritual Friend too much. The teacher will tell them to stop trying so hard because the most important part of Mettā is feeling the radiating—making a sincere wish for their Spiritual Friend's happiness and then feeling that happiness—not visualizing their friend.

If you are getting a headache or feeling pressure, you are *trying too hard*. Smile again and back off a little.

When you picture your spiritual friend, see them smiling and happy. Remember to keep a little smile on your lips for the entire meditation session. If you find yourself not smiling, then this will be a reminder to smile once again. Bring up another wish and send a kind feeling to your friend. Your face isn't used to smiling, so please be patient! Your cheeks might even hurt a little, but you will get used to it, and that uneasiness will pass.

Please don't criticize yourself for forgetting to smile. Critical thoughts about anything are unwholesome and lead to more suffering. If you see that you are coming down on yourself for forgetting to smile, then laugh at yourself for having such a crazy mind!

Understand that everyone has a crazy mind, and that it is okay to have this craziness. Laugh with yourself about it. This meditation is supposed to be fun, remember? Smile and laugh at getting caught again, then start all over with your object of meditation.

Life is a game to play, so keep everything light and have fun all of the time. It does take practice, but this is why you are doing this practice. Play with things and don't take them too seriously.

This *is* a serious meditation, but we do not want you to *be serious!* Your mind should not be too serious; rather, it should be light and uplifted. Smile, and if that does not work, then laughing a little bit should help you get back into that happier, alert state of mind.

You will use the same Spiritual Friend the entire time until the teacher says you can change. This may be a few days or weeks. If practicing on your own, get in touch with us via the website and let us help you; become part of our Yahoo discussion group). The more you can stay in the present—happy and content, feeling happiness with your Spiritual Friend—the sooner you will be able to move on to the next step of the meditation. You can always contact us through our website for guidance.

Once you have settled on a good Spiritual Friend, stay with that person. If you switch from one person to another, the practice won't be able to ripen or deepen. Sometimes meditators want to send Mettā to other people, or to all beings. This is just a subtle way your mind distracts you. You want to stay with the same friend in the beginning so that you can build your *collectedness*.

We replace the word "concentration" with the word *collectedness* to help clarify that we are not forcing our minds to stay on only one object of meditation in a forceful, fixed way. Rather, we want our mind to rest lightly on the object. If your mind wanders, use the 6Rs.

When there are no distractions, there is no need to exert any effort to keep your mind on its object. It just stays there by itself. That is really an amazing process to see.

Again, there may be times that some random thoughts and sensations arise while you are with your object of meditation but which are not strong enough to pull your attention away completely from it. When this happens, ignore those and stay with your meditation object. These thoughts and distractions will go away by themselves; there is no need to 6R them.

So let's review:

1. Sit for a minimum of thirty minutes (why is explained later).

2. *Begin* by radiating kind and happy thoughts and wishes to yourself for about *ten* minutes.

3. *Switch* to your one chosen Spiritual Friend for the remainder of your sitting—at least *twenty minutes*—and radiate kind and happy thoughts to them for the rest of the session. Stay with just the same Friend and do not switch to anything or anyone else, even if you think they "deserve" your attention. Such desires are just more distractions. The mind can be very sneaky!

4. *Use the 6Rs* to overcome distractions.

When the feeling of Mettā starts to become stronger, notice it and sink into it. Smile into it and let it develop by itself. If you find that you are subtly verbalizing the phrases and the verbalizing starts to cause some tightness, let go of the verbalization and just feel the wish. This will allow the feeling to grow even stronger. Stay with the feeling and just be in the moment without pushing or "leaning into" it.

This practice will take time to master. In a sense this is a kind of "not-doing"—you are not controlling or pushing the feeling, you are just gently directing it. If there is tension in your body from trying to send it out, then you are putting in too much effort. There should just be the wish for happiness, in the same way, you wish someone good luck on a journey. You stand and wave as they go—you don't stand and try to push a feeling out to them! Similarly, with Mettā meditation, you simply smile and wish this feeling of gentle Lovingkindness.

After doing the 6Rs and getting the hang of it, there will be a hindrance that arises. Finally, you 6R the last little bit of tension from it, and it disappears completely! Craving is eliminated for the first time. A small amount of craving is gone, never to arise again.

As a result of the hindrance disappearing Joy arises and, for the first time, you are experiencing the first *Tranquil Aware Jhāna*. There will be more to go as you progress along this path. As your practice advances, you will find that the joy is there. It can be goose bumps, thrills, or just excitement arising. A pleasant, tranquil feeling will follow it.

As you go deeper, your confidence gets stronger, and you understand that what you are doing is right. Also, you will notice there is a much deeper state of quiet in your mind than you have ever experienced before. It is like someone turned off the refrigerator you never even realized was on.

You might notice that you are not aware of parts of your body unless you direct your attention to them. This is a normal development as your body starts to lose tension and tightness, and this indicates progress.

Finally, as you get deeper, the feeling of Lovingkindness may rise into your head. Never try to control the feeling—if it wants to move there, then let it move.

Now you have become an advanced meditator.

When this happens, you will be ready for the next step of the meditation practice. This is what the rest of the book is about. You are now on your way through the Tranquil Aware Jhānas to the experience of awakening.

Forgiveness Meditation

There may be some of you who have difficulty bringing up and sustaining the feeling of loving-kindness — even after following all the instructions and guidance here. You may bring up a phrase, "May I be happy, may I be content" and this causes self-aversion or hatred to arise. "I don't deserve it, I am not a nice person," may arise in your mind. You try the 6R's, and it doesn't really work. There is no loving-kindness there, your heart just has no feeling and is dry and maybe hard.

You may find the practice of Forgiveness Meditation will help with this. We find now a not so small percentage of students benefit tremendously from switching to Forgiveness in which you radiate forgiveness to yourself and forgiving everything that comes up and as people come up, you forgive them until they forgive you.

You can find out more about this practice at the Dhamma Sukha website and in a book called *Forgiveness Meditation* by Bhante Vimalaraṁsi.

Forgiveness is about letting go of the past and softening our minds. Everyone can benefit from practicing forgiveness.

**In fact, the Forgiveness book is now included in this book at the back!

Walking Meditation

An important part of the Mettā practice is Walking Meditation. Please do not ignore it. You need to walk to keep your energy up, especially after longer sittings.

You can use Walking Meditation to build energy or uplift your mind before sitting if you feel sleepy or have low energy.

Sometimes, when your mind is distracted, walking will make it easier to calm a restless mind so that you can go back to sitting. Walking Meditation, on the other hand, can add energy to your sitting by getting your blood flowing.

Walking Meditation is a powerful meditation on its own but, in conjunction with Mettā Meditation, it helps you to incorporate Mettā into your everyday life and activities. Please do remember that this is an all-the-time practice.

Find a place to walk that is at least thirty paces and is straight and level. Walk at a normal pace as if you are taking a stroll in the park on a Sunday afternoon; not slowly like a turtle, but at a speed that is neither too fast nor too slow. Your eyes should be directed down in front of you six to ten feet ahead.

Do not put your attention on your feet. Instead, stay with your Spiritual Friend. Please do not look around, as that will distract you from your meditation. This is not a nature walk, but part of the actual practice where you are radiating kind and happy thoughts to your Spiritual Friend. As much as possible, stay with that practice the entire time you are walking. It is just like when you are sitting, with the only difference being that you are walking instead of sitting.

You may do this inside or outside as the weather permits. It is best done outside in the open air, but try to avoid the heat of direct sunlight. You can also walk inside, in a circular path around a room or down a hallway.

Some meditators make a lot of progress while walking — it can go quite deep. Do not take this instruction lightly as it is an important part of the practice. It also helps us learn how to practice Mettā in our everyday life where we are more active out in the world.

Walk for about fifteen to thirty minutes and never more than an hour, as this much walking will tire your body out. However, do walk at a good pace so that by the end of it, you will feel your heart pumping and you may be slightly out of breath. Then you can sit and be fully alert. Walking can bring calmness, clarity, *or* energy, depending on what you need at the time.

Keep it Going

Thirty minutes of meditation a day is the minimum to start. From our experience, it takes fifteen to twenty minutes to get the mind to settle down. Then you are giving yourself another ten productive minutes where you can truly watch and observe. Forty-five minutes is better.

Just the fact you are sitting and not moving permits the mind to calm down. The longer you sit, the more your mind will calm on its own, without you doing anything else. So sitting longer and not moving is vital to progress to deeper states.

On retreat, you will at first sit at least thirty minutes, walk fifteen minutes, then sit again, alternating like this for the whole day. Your sittings will naturally get longer and longer throughout the retreat and may eventually last as long as two to three hours.

In your daily life, sitting twice a day is very helpful. Once you're comfortable, try to stay completely still throughout the sitting period. If the mind insists on moving, 6R the desire to move. The 6Rs are very helpful in dissolving tension and finding deeper ease.

If pain arises, please watch *how* it arises. You can tell if the pain is genuine by noticing what happens when you get up from sitting. If the pain goes away very quickly, it is a "meditation pain," which is, in fact, a mental pain and is not caused by anything harmful. It is just a distraction. If it returns when you sit, try to remain still and 6R. If, when you get up, the pain lingers and stays with you, it is best not to sit that way in the future, because this would be actual physical pain manifesting.

If we try to get rid of painful or unpleasant feelings forcefully, whether mental or physical, we just add more greed and aversion to the mind. This fuels the vicious cycle of *Saṃsāra*. However, if we approach an unpleasant feeling openly and without taking it personally, we view these unwholesome qualities with *wholesome* awareness. This pure, clear awareness gradually melts that disturbing feeling. Moreover, you might notice the feeling linger, but your attitude toward it has changed.

If you get sleepy sitting inside, try sitting outside but not in the direct sun. The outdoors tends to wake you up. You can even try doing the walking practice backward after you walk forward thirty paces. Instead of turning around, just walk backward to the starting point.

Meditation and its benefits increase if you can continue to cultivate awareness throughout the day. Smile and send Mettā whenever you think of it. When you notice difficult feelings coming up, 6R them. Do this with a sense of fun and humor at just how crazy mind can be. If you get serious and try to control the mind, that is just more Craving. You may wear yourself out and become frustrated. So, do this lightly, but with as much continuity as possible.

Add Mettā to Everything

You can bring Lovingkindness into everything that you do. Generally, you will do your sitting at home, but you can also smile and radiate well-being and happiness to all beings when you are out and about. If you are just going out walking or shopping, you do not have to stay with a Spiritual Friend. Stay with a general feeling of Mettā.

Smile more. Notice and 6R emotional upsets that arise. When unwholesome states of mind arise, see them as opportunities. Let them be and bring up wholesome ones. This is the meaning of Right Effort in the Buddha's Noble Eightfold Path.

Progress and Jhāna

As you make progress with the meditation, you will see all kinds of new phenomena. Joy and other pleasant experiences will arise. Some of them will be really worth the price of admission!

The first time you truly and completely let go of a hindrance, you will have your first experience of the jhānic state and be on your way to going even deeper. You will start to be friends with fun stuff like Joy, Contentment, Equanimity, and more. Good times are on the way!

Brahmavihāras and Nibbāna

The Buddha talked about four divine qualities of mind that are particularly wholesome. They are called the *Brahmavihāras* and consist of Lovingkindness (*Mettā*), Compassion (*karuṇā*), Sympathetic Joy (*muditā*)—we actually prefer just Joy—and Equanimity (*upekkhā*). This is the practice you are starting now. You will gradually go through all these states very naturally as Mettā becomes quieter and turns to compassion and so on through joy to equanimity. You do not need to change the practice as you go—the states themselves will develop and arise on their own.

Once you become an advanced meditator, you just have to keep the meditation going. The Brahmavihāras develop naturally, one by one, without you having to bring up each of these states as its own separate meditation object. When the next state arises, then you take that state, whether it be compassion or joy as the feeling, to be the object of meditation and continue radiating that out now.

This is another important difference from how other practices have you develop Mettā. The Buddha taught that when the meditation is properly practiced, all four divine states arise on their own one after the other.[4] You will learn how to radiate any of these four states to all of the six directions and then to all directions at the same time.

As this happens, the *jhānas* will arise naturally on their own as well. The word jhāna is a loaded word. It has been translated in many different ways, but we refer to the jhānas as levels of understanding. We do not want to confuse them with their one-pointed absorption jhāna cousins. They are related, but these are ones in which the meditator keeps awareness of their body, whereas the others do not. The Buddha taught that the key to understanding Craving and distractions is to realize that mind *and* body are one process that cannot be separated. Tension and tightness are bodily processes, while thought and images are mental processes. We not only want to pay attention to the mind but also be aware of what is happening in the body and not ignore or repress this awareness through one-pointed focused concentration.

We call the jhānic states that we experience with this meditation the *Tranquil Aware Jhānas*. There are eight of them (four *rūpa* or "material" jhānas, and four *arūpa* or "immaterial" jhānas). Beyond the highest immaterial jhāna lies the experience of Nibbāna itself. Your mind will become so quiet that it just stops. When the mind comes

---

4   *Majjhima Nikāya, sutta 43:31, shows the progression of radiating into all directions starting with Lovingkindness.*

back from that cessation experience, it will be incredibly bright and clear, with no disturbance—like a blackboard with nothing on it.

At that point, when the next mental process arises, you will see with astonishing clarity every link and part of this process that we call life as it arises and passes away. This process is what the Buddha called Dependent Origination. There are twelve links in each moment of experience, and you will see how all of these arise and pass away. You will see how all of these dependently arise one upon the other.

When you see very deeply into this process, you will understand, at a profound personal level, that all of the "aggregates" that make up "you," or the "I," are actually impersonal and without any sort of enduring self or soul. This experience is so profound that Nibbāna will arise, and you will understand the true nature of all existence. You will have attained awakening in this very life. There will be so much relief!

Experiencing awakening (Nibbāna) happens for many people who follow these simple directions. It does not take years or decades. The Buddha said that this practice is "immediately effective." In the Satipaṭṭhāna Sutta of the Majjhima Nikāya, he says that this experience can take place in as little as seven years, or even seven days. It can truly happen that fast; we have seen it take place within a single eight-day retreat. So, start now, and you too can experience the initial stages of awakening. Just follow the instructions exactly!

Benefits of Lovingkindness

There are many benefits to practicing Lovingkindness meditation. In the suttas, it says that when you practice Mettā meditation, you go to sleep easily and sleep soundly. You have no nightmares. When you wake up, you awaken easily and quickly. People really like you! Animals like you. Your face becomes radiant and beautiful. You have good health. These are just a few of the benefits.

When you practice Lovingkindness, your mind also becomes clear and quiet, and your progress in the meditation is very fast.

Mettā in Daily Life

Continue to sit and practice. Listen to talks, read our books, and study more about the concepts surrounding this practice. There are many resources on our website.

When starting any new practice, it is usually best to immerse yourself in that practice, setting aside other practices you may have done in the past, until you understand the new practice deeply and thoroughly. Otherwise, you may be confused with the various opinions and practices that are out there.

Remember that we are not basing our teaching on views or opinions, but rather on the study of the suttas themselves and the direct experience of the meditation practice. We invite you to follow this path as well.

The best way to experience deep immersion into Tranquil Wisdom Insight Meditation is to come for a retreat or if you cannot get away, do an online retreat with us. Check our website for more information.

Once you master staying with the Spiritual Friend, there are more instructions for breaking down barriers and radiating the feeling of Mettā in all directions. The teacher will give you those directions and advise you when you are ready. This is where the practice of the Brahmavihāras really takes off.

More phenomena will arise, and a teacher can guide you based on your progress. There are more steps in the practice, but they are advanced and are for another book.

For now, master the ability to stay with your Spiritual Friend perfectly and then contact us, or just come and do a retreat with us.

Again, when you are outside moving around in daily life, remember to smile and radiate Mettā to all beings. Use Right Effort to recondition your mind. Bring up the wholesome quality of Lovingkindness instead of allowing whatever "ho-hum" mind is there.

Stuck in a long line at the checkout line? Radiate Mettā. It is a tough job being a cashier at a store, so smile at the cashier and be friendly.

Traffic bogged down, and you just can't move? Rather than getting upset, radiate Mettā to your fellow drivers. 6R your upset mind and replace it with a wholesome, uplifted mind. Put a CD in the car player and listen to a Dhamma talk to learn more about the Eightfold Path of the Buddha, rather than wasting your own time ho-humming your way through life.

Share what you have learned with other people, and let them benefit from your practice. Pay this practice forward once you understand it. Don't proselytize! Just talk about what happened to you in your own words. How is it helping you be happier? Be *the Buddha* rather than a *Buddhist!*

Can't find a sitting group in your area? Start your own. As soon as you find one more person, you have a group! Meditate for at least thirty minutes, listen to a talk, have some tea and discuss what you have learned. Right there, you have just created your own sitting group!

Little by little, like drops of water filling a cup, you will soon come to supreme awakening. It is possible to do this right now. The Buddha showed us the way. Just follow the instructions *exactly*!

Now, let's get into the Jhāna states and see, ultimately, how Nibbāna arises.

Chapter Six: 1st Jhāna — Joy

When your attention stays with the feeling of loving-kindness and your spiritual friend, for about three to five minutes, then joy will arise; congratulations you have arrived at the first tranquil aware jhāna!

How does a jhāna arise? First, a distraction arises, fueled by one or more of the hindrances. Whatever it happens to be — greed, hatred, or restlessness — as you let it go, relax, and come back to your object of meditation, the hindrance begins to weaken. When a hindrance arises, it is not your enemy to fight with. Rather, it is a friend for you to invite in, allowing it to show you where your attachments are.

Every time you 6R the hindrance, it grows weaker. Why? Because you have released the craving which is embedded in the distraction arising. Finally, you do one last 6R process, and the hindrance *completely* disappears. It just has no further energy. From this release and resulting relief, the first jhāna arises, and mind enters into a pure state. When the hindrance runs out of energy, you have a real sense of relief. You feel joy arising, which is an exciting, happy feeling. You will feel light in both your mind and body. Quite nice!

Hindrances are constantly tightening down on our awareness and pulling our mood down. They lead to a lot of frowning and stress. Now you see the beginning of real happiness arising. It is like you have been in a coarse, painful state your whole life and someone just switches it off.

You feel joy (*pīti*) in the head, in the chest, and throughout the body. It may feel full or warm or light. It may be like bubbles popping. It may be subtle or, for some, it may be felt as more extreme joy. There might be some mental and visual activities, or even fireworks going on behind your closed eyes. This will settle down after a period of time, a few hours or a day. The mental state will be energized and joyful, and it will definitely be a pleasant feeling. There will be no hindrances at this time. This is a big relief. Right after the joy fades away, mind will become very tranquil and comfortable; this is called happiness or sukha. Mind just stays on its object with almost no effort at all. You have never experienced happiness and clarity like this before.

I will insert some comments from past students taking a physical or online retreat with this practice.

" I was able to generate loving-kindness and radiate the feeling to my spiritual friend. Within a few seconds, I felt an overwhelming wave of joy. It was like my spiritual friend was radiating mettā back to me. I cried out of joy.... Again, I returned to my meditation object (spiritual friend), but again I felt the wave of joy, this time I just felt tremendously grateful." E.M. California

What is joy? *Excitement and a happy feeling* are the nature of joy at this beginning stage. A man in a desert who is dying of thirst, spots in the distance an oasis and a pool of cool water. He becomes very excited and happy. This is the feeling of joy. The moment he sees it, joy arises. This is what happens in the first jhāna.

The joy in the first jhāna is followed by a feeling of tranquility and relaxation. You are still in the first jhāna, but it is changing. You will feel this. You *will* be smiling and radiant. The jhāna will last for a while until another hindrance pops up.

Sometimes the joy is not strong, and meditators are not sure they have achieved anything, so they don't mention it. On a retreat, over the course of the daily interviews, the teacher will inquire about what is happening to you. They will ask you, "Is there any joy?" The teacher will get a hint when you say you can stay on your meditation object for a longer period of time.

Let's follow this simile a bit longer and do a brief explanation of the next three jhanas so you can see how the practice develops.

As you continue meditating, your joy from the first jhāna will deepen. There will arise a feeling of strong confidence. This is a quieter, deeper joy where both mind and body become very light, almost like floating. Both mind and body become very tranquil, comfortable, and peaceful. This is the second jhāna.

When the man finally arrives at the pool of cool water and jumps in, the temperature of the water is just right. Both his mind and body kind of give a gentle sigh of relief — this is where he experiences happiness and contentment. This is the feeling of happiness (*sukha*) and a developing sense of mental balance that occurs in the third jhāna.

This happiness will fade away just leaving a stability of mind that is a feeling of equanimity (*upekkhā*), which is the fourth jhāna.

The Suttas Explain the Jhānas

The Anupada Sutta, "One By One As They Occurred" Number 111, from the Majjhima Nikāya (MN), explains the entire process and all the characteristics of the jhanas up to the attainment of Nibbāna. I will use this sutta to explain throughout the rest of the book the jhānas "one by one," and the subsequent progress to awakening.

The sutta MN 111 starts: "And the states in the first jhāna — the thinking and examining thought, the joy, the happiness, and the unification of mind;"[ix]

You have let go of a hindrance, and joy arises. There are five different kinds of joy. The first kind of joy is like goosebumps; it is there for just a moment, and then it goes away. The next kind of joy is like a flash of lightning; it's very intense for a very short period, and then that fades away. The third kind of joy is as if you are standing in the ocean and you have these waves of joy washing over you; it's just wave after wave. These three kinds of joy can happen to anyone for any reason when the conditions are right.

The last two types of joy only arise from mental development. The fourth kind of joy is called uplifting joy. You feel very light in your mind and light in your body. You feel very happy, and there is excitement in it. This is the joy of the first and second jhānas.

The fifth and last kind of joy is called all-pervading joy. It just kind of comes out of everywhere; it bubbles out all over and pervades your whole mind. (This kind of joy is also called the awakening factor of Joy.) This is the joy you feel when you attain Nibbāna.

So, the fourth type of joy arises, and right after that, when it fades away, you feel very tranquil and comfortable in your mind and in your body. This feeling is what the Buddha calls *sukha*, which is the Pāli word for happiness. Your mind does not wander very much in your meditation; it doesn't get lost. There is still the *thinking and examining mind*; you still can internally verbalize thoughts about your experience. You are still thinking, but now only wholesome states are there — though it is still a bit "noisy" as compared to the states that come later. You are not carried away by unwholesome thoughts. There is no craving now. Thoughts that occur are thinking and examining thoughts that have to do with what you are feeling right now, in the present.

You feel very peaceful and collected. In Pāli, the word for this state is *ekaggatā*. And if you look up the word in the Pāli dictionary, *ekagga* means tranquility, peacefulness, and stillness of mind. It doesn't mean one-pointed or absorption, but rather, collected and unified.

The sutta explains there are *five factors* in the first jhāna: thinking and examining thought, joy, happiness, and unification of mind. The sutta goes on to explain what else is there:

MN: the contact, feeling, perception, volition, and mind…

The five aggregates — body, feeling, perception, formations (volitions), and consciousness — are also present in this jhāna. This means that all the foundations of mindfulness are there and will be observed. These comprise who you are, and you can see all the aggregates there without the veil of craving. You see with "little dust in your eyes."

Then the sutta says:

"[T]he enthusiasm, decision, energy, mindfulness, equanimity, and attention — these states were defined by him one by one as they occurred; known to him those states arose, known they were present, known they disappeared.

What are we talking about here? We are talking about impermanence. You begin to see impermanence while you are in the jhāna; you see these things arise and pass away one by one as they occur. The factors listed in the sutta don't necessarily follow the order that they're given here; they come up whenever they're going to come up. These are the first initial insights or understandings (vipassanā in Pāli) that arise for you.

MN: "He understood thus: 'So indeed, these states, not having been, come into being; having been, they vanish.'"

An obstacle that sometimes comes here is that some meditators will try to 6R the joy and happiness that arises, thinking that they might get attached to it. They think they should try to suppress it and not allow it to be there.

You do not need to do this, you should let this happy feeling be there with full acceptance, but still go back to your spiritual friend and continue the meditation. This joy is a fruit of the practice and is wholesome. Just let it be. It is okay for you to have joy. It's okay to be happy! It's kind of a new idea to let happiness be there and not push it away. And to even develop it and keep the happy state going which is the last part of Right Effort.

If you have excessive thoughts and start thinking about what just happened (the joy arising), you can 6R those thoughts and let them go, as you've started to take the joy personally and become *attached* to it. That is craving, and that keeps us on the Wheel of Saṃsāra — the Wheel of Suffering. Again, you should never push the joy away; just 6R it, allow it but don't get involved in it. It is a wholesome state, and wholesome states are what we are striving for.

The Buddha said it is part of Right Effort to notice an unwholesome state and bring up a wholesome state. He didn't say to replace a wholesome state with an "even more wholesome" state. Wholesome is wholesome. Just let it be. It is enough.

Gradually, this happy feeling will subside. Or possibly it may come up again and again over a few days — it will be there as long as it is there.

There was a fellow who had tears rolling down his cheeks, and everyone thought he was upset. It was joy and, finally, he was told just to get a towel and let the tears fall on that. No need to make it stop. It will stop on its own.

After some time, you will lose this happy feeling, and the hindrances will come back. You will certainly start to think, "Oh if I could just get that experience again!" This is craving and should be 6R'd.

Often, at this stage, if you fail to follow the teacher's instructions to 6R, you might go around trying to figure out how to get that state back. And you won't!

Subsequently, you might "crash and burn, " and the next day you will be frustrated at not being able to bring back the experience. Some meditators are "smarter" than others: they just go back to the meditation as they had practiced it before and continue following the instructions. Some may take an extra day, and that's okay. We all have to learn. Wanting something only creates frustration in mind. We need to 6R that too.

—*Meditation Instruction:*

On a retreat, the teacher will now give you further instructions. For those of you using this book on your own, please pay attention to this next instruction.

After you feel this joyful feeling arising, you can *drop* the verbalization for your spiritual friend — "May you be happy," "May you be peaceful," etc. Just feel the wish for their happiness without mentally verbalizing. There is no further need for the phrases as they may cause tension and tightness in your head — and we certainly don't wish to create more tightness.

This is a sign of progress in your meditation. Your thoughts have quieted down, and you are starting to experience the quieting presence of the second jhāna. More about this jhāna in the next chapter.

The teacher will not tell you what jhāna you are in until you have gotten to the fourth jhāna. At that stage, you will have a firm grip on the technique and how to 6R distractions. You understand that these are just levels of understanding and tranquility that you are going through. As your meditation progresses, you start to develop some equanimity and won't care so much what state you are in. At that point, the teacher will tell you that you have become an "advanced" meditator and congratulate you on your progress — but there is more to do.

Walking Meditation and the Jhānas

Walking is an important part of this meditation, as it helps to sustain energy, overcome sloth and torpor, and maintain health generally when you are sitting for long periods of time. However, one of the most important purposes of walking meditation is to enable you to practice integrating TWIM meditation into your daily life. The purpose of meditation is to bring change to all parts of your life all the time, not just while you are sitting. Walking meditation will help you to accomplish this.

While you were sitting, you were staying with your Spiritual Friend and 6Ring distractions. Now, the only difference is that you are walking, just strolling normally, and keeping your mind on radiating kind thoughts to your spiritual friend, in the same way, when you were sitting (see *A Guide to TWIM* for an in-depth discussion of how to do walking meditation.)

One of the mistakes many people make when they are talking about jhanas is to think that a jhana only arises while you're doing your *sitting* meditation. However, you can take any one of these jhanas and stay with it while you get up and do your walking meditation. You can also be in this state when you're washing the dishes; you could even be taking a bath or standing in the checkout line at the store. Staying with your object of meditation while you are walking and during all your activities will help you to progress further.

Unlike being in absorption jhana, any one of the tranquil aware jhanas can arise during your daily activities. This is one of the reasons that you keep your meditation going all the time. It doesn't matter what you are doing — it's all part of the practice.

Everything you do is practice. If you train in this way, then you will make progress. Be aware of what your mind is doing all the time. Remember to stay with the meditation practice as much as possible. That's the first part of mindfulness — remembering to practice. Remember what? Observing mind's attention moving from one thing to another.

Chapter Seven: 2nd Jhāna — Noble Silence

MN-111 section 5. "Again, monks, with the stilling of [thinking and examining thought], Sāriputta entered and abided in the second jhāna, which has self-confidence and [stillness] of mind without thinking and examining thought, with joy and happiness born of collectedness."

The joy that arises in the second jhāna is stronger than the first and deeper; you feel much lighter in your mind, much lighter in your body. Sometimes it feels like you are floating in your chair. There are students that say they felt so light that they had to open their eyes because they thought they were going to hit the ceiling. This is the uplifting type of joy from attaining a meditative state.

The happiness you experience is a comfortable peacefulness. There is a calm feeling in your mind and in your body.

Mind quiets down, like when a refrigerator turns off. You hadn't even noticed it was on, and then the compressor clicks off. It's a level of quiet that you never thought possible.

Confidence appears. You feel you are really starting to understand the meditation. You feel like you have no more doubts about how to do this practice. You are starting to understand the 6Rs.

When you're in the first jhāna, you can still have thoughts, and you can still have thinking and examining mind which means a wholesome observing mind that is thinking about the experience.

When you enter the second jhāna, this is where true, *noble silence* begins. This is real noble silence. It is not writing notes on retreat instead of talking all the while your mind is speeding along. It is noble silence because your internal verbalizing has essentially stopped.

While you are in this state, if you try to make a wish like, "May I be happy" this will cause more tension and more phrases mentally repeated will cause your head to get tight. You then are advised to stop making verbal wishes as it explains below.

—*Meditation Instruction:*

Again, for meditators using this book as a guide, now let go of internal verbalizing of the wishes. Simply *wish* loving-kindness for your spiritual friend. Bring up the feeling without the phrases. When you are in the 2nd jhāna, and you repeat phrases you will find it causes tension in your head and mind and you can't do it comfortably. That is your signal to let go of internal verbalization.

Chapter Eight: 3rd Jhāna
— Happiness

MN:111 section 7. "Again, monks, with the fading away of joy, Sāriputta abided in equanimity, and mindful, and fully aware, still feeling pleasure [happiness] with the body, still feeling happiness with the body, he entered upon and abided in the third jhāna, on account of which noble ones announce: 'He has a pleasant abiding who has equanimity and is mindful.'"

When you get into the third jhāna, you start losing body awareness. This is a way to mark your progress. You'll be sitting and all of a sudden you think, "I don't feel my hands," or "I don't feel my leg," or "my shoulder disappeared" (unless you consciously put your attention there, and then you feel them). You feel very tranquil, and sometimes it can be a heavy, yet pleasant feeling. This is a sign that you are starting to *truly understand* the use of the 6Rs.

This is not a state of absorption where if someone pokes you, you would not feel it. This is a state where your attention is not on the body unless there is contact — it can be an outside force demanding your attention as in the teacher calls you, or someone taps your shoulder.

Whenever the attention is drawn somewhere, it is because there is craving there. When a feeling arises, you want to feel it and check it out. There is a little craving in every part of the mental stream. If a pleasant feeling arises, craving arises, and we launch into liking or disliking that feeling. Then the thoughts and stories come up about the feeling; what the feeling is about, the perception that comes with the feeling, and the story about the feeling. Again, we 6R and continue.

When you get into the third jhāna, you let go of a lot of mental tension. When you let go of that mental tension, you start letting go of physical tension as well. Bhante said that one meditator came to him and told him she felt just like her head was sitting on the floor. There was nobody there, just a head rolling around.

"At one point I couldn't feel my extremities. Not because they were asleep or anything. They just disappeared. I was much less distracted and was able to focus more. I studied the 6 Rs more and was able to really use them when needed." C.G. Missouri

A loud noise like a motorcycle might be heard outside, and you know that this happened. You have a balanced mind about it. There is much more equanimity in the third jhāna. Sounds don't make your mind shake; they don't make your mind flutter. Your mind just says: "Okay, there was a sound. Never mind, relax, come back to your object of meditation." There is this strong balance that occurs. You feel more comfortable than you've ever felt, very much at ease in your body. Bodily tension has all but disappeared.

Whereas in the first and second jhānas you had joy coming up, now it starts to fade away. You will ask, "Where has the joy gone? I like that. I want it back!"

You have gone beyond that coarser level of excitement and arrived at a deeper, more content state. The word used here is *happiness* (sukha) along with contentment. This is not joy anymore. Sometimes the student needs to be reassured, "It's okay not to have joy. This is progress. Your mind is going deeper."

Mind becomes very tranquil and very unified, not in a one-pointed way where the senses are shut out, but it stays on one object.

It just sits there, and there is no need for control. It is *happy* there. Everything is okay.

You are starting to see with a quieter mind. You can notice when mental movements first start to arise. You can let them go and relax. You'll start to see that mind begins to flutter a little bit, and then it flutters faster and faster, and then it gets completely distracted away. You'll begin to observe how that process works. When you first notice this fluttering, if you relax right then, your mind stays on your object of meditation. As you go deeper, your wandering mind is 6r'd sooner.

Mettā Takes You to the Fourth Jhāna

In the Saṃyutta Nikāya, there is a section on loving-kindness meditation that refers to the factors of awakening. This sutta is a real revelation because it is talking about practicing loving-kindness in the fourth jhāna. The reason that this is a revelation is that it is widely held that loving-kindness can only take you to the *third jhāna*. But, there it is in the sutta[x] talking about experiencing the feeling of mettā in the fourth jhāna.

The suttas disagree with the Visuddhi Magga about this. In reading the sutta "Accompanied by Loving-kindness" No.46 section 54 (4) from the Saṃyutta Nikāya, it says that, on the other hand, mettā, or loving-kindness, goes to the *fourth jhāna*; *compassion* goes to the base of infinite space, the first arūpa jhāna; *joy* goes to the base of infinite consciousness, the second arūpa jhāna; and *equanimity* goes to the base of nothingness, the third arūpa jhāna.

The practice that is being taught here is not only loving-kindness; it is the complete practice of the *Brahmavihāras*. There are four "abodes or divine abidings of Brahma" that make up the brahmavihāras which are Loving-kindness (Mettā), Compassion (Karuṇā), Joy (Muditā) and Equanimity (Upekkhā). Loving-kindness is the first part of this larger system that eventually leads to the experience of Nibbāna.

The Loving-kindness meditation that we are talking about here is not just a *side* meditation to help us calm down after a long day at the office, or to prepare for our meditation on the breath, it is a powerful system in its own right as part of the Brahmavihāra meditation path and does, indeed, culminate in full awakening.

Bhante Vimalaraṁsi talks about some of his Malaysian students who would come off a difficult Vipassanā retreat and request to take a mettā retreat with him. He said that they said their minds had been hardened by those retreats and that they needed to return to a more balanced, happy state.

Who could think that a method that Buddha taught would cause hardness, not lead directly to the goal, and need mettā to recover from it? Were these other retreats being taught in the way the Buddha instructed? If they had added the relax step, then this could have been avoided.

Mettā is a very important practice that the Buddha taught which can take you directly to Nibbāna. That misunderstanding that it will *not* take you to the goal needs to be corrected. Mettā is just the first part of the Brahmavihāras system that you experience as you go deeper into your practice. It automatically leads to the other three vihāras, but you have to continue the practice. Mettā is, indeed, the doorway to the unconditioned.

After all the definition of Right Effort is to 1)Recognize there is an unwholesome state, 2)to let go of that unwholesome state, 3)bring up a wholesome state — 4)keep it going. Four parts. And what is more wholesome than Mettā. You just keep it going and it will lead you to Nibbāna with no other methods needed. This is what it says right in the texts themselves.

Chapter Nine: 4th Jhāna
— The Beautiful

MN:111 section 9. "Again monks, with the abandoning of pleasure and pain, and with the previous disappearance of joy and grief, Sāriputta entered upon and abided in the fourth jhāna, which has neither pain nor pleasure and purity of mindfulness due to equanimity."

In the fourth jhāna, the loving-kindness energy moves from the chest and heart area, up to your head; it is like the feeling of mettā is starting to radiate from the top of the head. The spiritual friend smiles back, and there is no more warmth in the chest area from the loving-kindness.

In no circumstances should you try to push the feeling back down to your heart area again. It should be allowed to go where it wants to based on the sincerity of your loving-kindness.

Some meditators make the mistake of trying to make a feeling arise by focusing on their heart and chest area. That's not right. They should be bringing up sincere wishes of loving-kindness which they really mean and honestly believe. Then the feeling appears on its own, and it goes where it needs to.

In the 4th jhāna, the contentment turns into a deeper peaceful feeling, full of equanimity; it is a nonreactive state of balance. It doesn't mean that there cannot be a painful or a pleasurable feeling arising; it means that it doesn't make your mind shake. You see it for what it is, and you have this beautiful balance towards it. The fourth jhāna in some texts is called "The Beautiful."

"Ultra-strong balance. When I finished the meditation, I was blissed out - not intense joy - just very relaxed. A strong feeling of equanimity, totally still and silent, and lots of automatic smiling.

In the meditation itself, it was very easy to see the people I sent loving-kindness to, smile. The loving-kindness stayed in the head and once again I lost perception or sense of body consciousness. Just felt floaty, light and expansive. S.D. California

You don't notice sensations arising inside your body, but you do notice external contact. If an ant walks on you, you know it. You have such balance that nothing bothers you. A mosquito comes around, and he bites you; it's okay, so what, no big deal. Mind is in balance to all feeling. In the fourth jhāna, pain in your body will disappear as your mind no longer reacts with an "I don't like it" mind. Of course, when the next hindrance occurs you can fall out of that state, and the pain will come back.

Also, there are reports of golden light pervading your mind and this wonderful feeling pouring out of the top of the head.

In the fourth jhāna, because there is contact with the ground while you're walking, you will feel sensation from your feet. This is because of contact with the ground. Bodily sensations will not draw your attention. Your sense of self-awareness will have moved up to your head area now.

You have now given up your beginner status. You're not a novice anymore. You've become an advanced meditator. But, interestingly, you are balanced and not over-excited with that. It's just more self-discovery, and you don't get a "big head" about it, whereas at the first jhāna you might have thought you were pretty good. Now it is just another step on the path with no looking back.

Advancing — Breaking Down the Barriers

You are now told that you have developed the meditation skills to a higher level. You are told this so that you have confidence in the practice and gain more enthusiasm. Previously, you weren't informed of what was happening because it would just lead to more mental wanderings. Now that you have some more equanimity and your mind has calmed, you are told where you are day by day what exact jhāna you are in, as it happens if you ask about it. You see that sutta MN 111 is real. And, like Sāriputta, you are just watching the progress step-by-step as it occurs.

—Meditation Instruction:

Now, you are to change your spiritual friend. You have completed the practice to this point and have now advanced. It's time to move ahead.

Let go of the friend you have been working with and change to the people listed below. Go through each group one at a time until you see them smiling and happy.

- Pick *three more spiritual friends* (any gender, living, and not a family member), and one-by-one radiate loving-kindness to them until they smile back or you feel there is a connection of loving-kindness with them.

- *Four living family members* (either male or female — gender no longer matters). One-by-one radiate loving-kindness to them until they smile back.

- *Four neutral people* (either male or female). One-by-one radiate loving-kindness to them until they smile back. A neutral person is a casual acquaintance that you occasionally see, like the bus driver or the cashier at the store. You don't really know them, but you say "Hello" every now and then.

- *Enemies* are last. Send mettā to any troublesome people, whoever arises. Enemies are those people we don't like. We may hold a grudge, or we know they don't care for us. It might be public figures or any person who comes to your mind when you do this. One by one, radiate mettā to people who pop into your mind until you can't think of anyone else.

If hatred, or even dislike, arises while radiating mettā to an enemy, go back to a neutral person until you can let go of the aversion and come back to that feeling of loving-kindness. Then begin again. Radiate mettā to your enemy and continue until that hostile energy is dissipated and they smile back. It doesn't have to be that deep — just have a friendly feeling for them. Or even a neutral feeling in which they don't bother you. Remember: everyone has some good qualities. You can focus on those.

You can do the process above in as little as twenty to thirty minutes. But you should spend no more than an hour on this.

If you cannot get beyond this step, then perhaps some forgiveness meditation will be suggested by the teacher. Information and directions for Forgiveness Meditation may be found on the Dhamma Sukha website and practiced from the book on this topic by Bhante Vimalaraṁsi. Forgiveness is a very powerful practice by itself and is highly recommended to everyone, but especially to those who cannot bring up a genuine feeling of loving-kindness for any of these groups of people.

"This morning I did my first Breaking Down the Barriers sitting. It went so well. I saw everyone smiling at me pretty quickly. Then I got to my "enemies" There is a woman I'm quite jealous of. I forgave myself for it. I wished her love, peace and happiness. Then I saw the smile. The second one is my niece's husband. I've never seen him smile in real life, so I don't even know what that would look like. But, as I was wishing peace for both of us, it felt like a lightning bolt went through my heart. I knew then I am wrong for the hate I'm feeling toward him. Only love can beat hate." C.G. Missouri

Radiating to the Six Directions

—Meditation Instruction:

After the process of breaking down the barriers is complete, you will report back to the teacher. Or if you are working on your own then simply continue below.

You will be now instructed to radiate loving-kindness from the head — not from the "third eye" or forehead but from the area in the middle of or the top of your head. You radiate to each of the six directions — Forward, Backward, Right, Left, Above, and Below — for five minutes apiece; that is thirty minutes total.

For the rest of the sitting, you then radiate to all beings in all directions at once, to the whole universe without limitations. Sit and glow with this feeling of loving-kindness and let it warm the whole cosmos and beyond. Like a candle, let the feeling radiate to all beings. Don't push or force; just let it radiate and see it just going out by itself. Now the fun begins!

"I was completely immersed. At one point there was no "me." All I saw was the light going in all directions. It was like a fountain going up, down, and in all directions. I was so absorbed when my timer went off I jumped. My husband said I looked like I was radiating, full of joy and peace." C.G. Missouri

You should sit for more than one hour if you can. You are encouraged to sit even longer if you are comfortable. Don't stop when you feel good or think you have made progress. Go longer. Don't stop if you get edgy or want to quit. Try another five minutes just to see if you can do it. Many times a few more minutes will get you through that short period of restlessness.

Radiating the four *Brahmavihāras* successively, as they arise, to all directions will now be your practice into the highest states of the meditation. Please note that I am describing the technique as it is presented in the texts. I am only explaining the texts here and not creating a "new" sort of meditation. You are now practicing the Brahmavihāra practice exactly as it is described and taught by the Buddha in the texts.

This practice of mettā and the rest of the Brahmavihāras are actually mentioned much more frequently: in twelve suttas in the Majjhima Nikāya versus the breath or Anapanasati practice which is only found in four suttas.[xi] Which one do you think the Buddha taught more often? He did appear to favor the Brahmavihāras over the breath practice.

Bhante Vimalaramsi states that mettā is six times quicker than breath and gets you to the goal much faster. He says it takes six weeks for someone to experience jhāna with breath versus a week (or less) with mettā. This has been our experience, and thus we always recommend mettā first. He *will* teach breath to certain personality types that have a hard time with the feeling of loving-kindness. But, he does add the relax or tranquilize step.

Chapter Ten: The Base of Infinite Space — Compassion

The Buddha taught that there are four major jhānas, but he broke up the fourth jhāna into four more parts.

The suttas call the last four parts "bases" or "realms." We will primarily use the term "bases" but will shift back and forth at times between "base" and "arūpa jhāna" just to make sure you understand the connection.

Now you have arrived at the *arūpa* or "immaterial" jhānas. The first four jhānas are called *rūpa* or "material" jhānas. *Rūpa* means "realm of the body," and *arūpa* means "realm of mind;" more precisely, the *ā* in *arūpa* means "no:" so "not of the body."

The word "realm" is also used in addition to base for these higher parts of the fourth jhāna. This is because the Buddha stated that if one were to attain any of these four jhānas (including the four immaterial realms), then the power (*merit*) of that act would cause them to be reborn into a realm of existence that corresponds to the meditation level attained.[5] There are thirty-one planes of existence, and the jhāna based Brahma realms are the highest, most pleasant, and longest lasting. The higher the jhāna, the longer the lifetime in that corresponding realm and the more sublime the state.

---

[5] *Even if the meditator attains a jhāna just once in this lifetime, then they will be reborn into at least that corresponding jhāna realm. The act of attaining a jhāna is so powerful that it temporarily wipes out all evil karmic results except for the five heinous acts: killing either one's mother or father, killing an Arahant, causing a schism in the order, or wounding a Buddha. One supporting reference is found for this in the Saṃyutta Nikāya. SN 42.8: The Conch Blower" P. 1340 http://www.accesstoinsight.org/tipitaka/sn/sn42/sn42.008.than.html*

MN:111 section 11. "Again, monks, with the complete surmount-ing of [gross] perceptions of form, with the disappearance of [gross] perceptions of sensory impact, aware that 'space is infi-nite,' Sāriputta entered upon and abided in the base of infinite space.

This means you have surmounted the physical and now are entering the subtler mental realms. You are no longer paying attention to the five senses and are paying attention to what's in your mind only.

You start feeling a quieter loving-kindness now. You will realize that there is less warmth, less movement of the mettā; it is softer, like cotton. This is *Karuṇā* or Compassion. You have gone beyond the coarser state of loving-kindness and entered a more sublime, tranquil state.

You report back that the feeling of loving-kindness has no limit but is very big. It is as immense as the sky; your head feels like it gets larger. You feel like things are expanding outward. Maybe you feel as if the floor drops away and you are suspended in space. You may even feel like you are flying up into space.

This is a very pleasurable kind of feeling. It is "pretty awesome!" There is a continuous expansion outward — there is no center-point to be seen. There may be an exclamation of "*Oh wow!*" when explaining this delightful state to the teacher!

"Wow! As I progressed through the four meditation sittings today, each an hour or so long, it was like the spaciousness became larger, larger, and larger... I did the radiating of mettā for the five minutes in each of the six directions and then radiated outward throughout the rest of the meditation to all six directions at the same time. The sphere of mettā grew in size and just kept growing without stop-ping. The mettā itself also transformed - it was magnetic, as if in-

tensifying, and creating a strong energetic forcefield. Floating feeling intensified. Never felt such spaciousness and expansiveness before. There was insight into how awareness of feeling and perceptions arose and ceased infinitely and how "I" was not in control...
S.D., California

—Meditation Instruction:

You will now change from mettā to compassion as your new object of meditation. You expand this new feeling outward with no limits, to the six directions, as you have been doing with loving-kindness. Begin each meditation session radiating compassion for five minutes in each direction, and then radiate compassion to all beings in all directions at the same time for the remainder of the sitting. Loving-kindness has now automatically switched to the state of compassion!

Bhante Vimalaraṁsi tells us that this is the state that so many teachers refer to when they talk about the Buddha's infinite compassion. Bhante's opinion is that when the Buddha refers to compassion, the state that he is talking about is the base of infinite space or the first arūpa jhāna. It is not just a general state of caring or nurturing, but actually the jhānic state of compassion.

Bhante further explains that the Buddha did this practice every morning — getting into the jhāna of infinite space with compassion as his object of meditation. From this state, the Buddha would then survey the world for people who needed his compassion and were ready to understand his teachings. He would then go to them and instruct them in the Dhamma. He saw people who *had little dust in their eyes* and were ready to attain awakening.

MN:111 section 12. "And the states in the base of infinite space —
the perception of the base of infinite space and the unification of
mind; the contact, feeling, perception, volition, and mind.

You still experience the five aggregates, even though you're in an arūpa or mental jhāna. This says that you're still practicing the four foundations of mindfulness even while you are in the arūpa jhāna state.

You are now in a mental realm and awareness of your body has faded away unless there is contact. Notice that the sutta quoted above no longer includes experiencing pleasure *in the body*. Now you are told *you have no body*! So please don't pay attention to it anymore — 6R any tugs and pulls back into any awareness of the body. Now, you know your body is still there, sitting quietly, but your awareness is very much focused on mind.

MN:111 section 12 cont. [T]he enthusiasm, decision, energy, mindfulness, equanimity, and attention — these states were defined by him one by one as they occurred; known to him those states arose, known they were present, known they disappeared. He understood thus: ...and with the cultivation of that attainment, he confirmed that there is [still more].

—Meditation Instruction:

Continue sending your compassion to the six directions to see how it expands outward. The Brahmavihāra meditation develops in sequence through the four divine abidings — *automatically*. These states will arise on their own when you are ready. Don't bring them up — they will come up. Just keep going and see what happens next.

Chapter Eleven: The Base of Infinite Consciousness — Joy

MN:111 section 13. "Again, monks, by completely surmounting the base of infinite space, aware that 'consciousness is infinite,' Sāriputta entered upon and abided in the base of infinite consciousness.

This is a fascinating state. For one thing, the compassionate feeling automatically changes again to a feeling of altruistic joy. But that's not as clear a definition as it could be. It is a feeling that's very different from the compassion experienced previously. It is a feeling that Bhante prefers to call just *joy* or *joyfulness.*

Whereas before, joy was an exciting type of joy (pīti), now it becomes sublime and tranquil. This is *pīti* vs *muditā*. Regardless, you now go from a feeling of compassion to a feeling of joy.

—Meditation Instruction:

Now you start radiating joy in all directions instead of compassion. Joy is now your object of meditation.

What happens is, your awareness starts to be so good and so sharp, you begin to see individual consciousnesses arise and pass away continually. You see firsthand how truly impermanent everything is. There's no doubt in your mind anymore that everything just comes into existence and then fades away.

Sometimes, your eyes just pop open – there can be so much energy. If you try to close them they just stay open, so you just let them be open.

"The arising of awareness was automatic, and its ceasing too was automatic. It was all impersonal and uncontrollable. The sense of "I" disappeared and reappeared over and over and over. There were moments where awareness ceased completely -- there was nothing in between the arising and ceasing. The "lapse" in awareness grew in frequency and length as well as far as I could tell, but as soon as I saw this, I was back to seeing the arising and ceasing and then the spaciousness. When I finished the final sitting meditation, my mind was still, clear, and sharp. Mind and emotions never felt so pristine, calm and pure before."

"Nothing I can say here except excellent!" S.D., Calif

After you sit with this insight into impermanence and impersonality for a little while, something interesting happens. Some students report: "Well yes, I see all these consciousnesses: the eye, the ear, the nose, the tongue, the body, and mind; I see these consciousnesses arise and pass away, and it's really *tiresome*."

What you see now is not only impermanence but suffering. And you're seeing there's nobody home, there's no control over this process, it happens all by itself. You see *anicca* (impermanence), *dukkha* (suffering), and *anattā* (non-self) up close and personal while you're in the arūpa jhānas. In Buddhism, these are the three signs of existence. Anything that exists has this nature, and now you see it. It isn't on a thinking level but in a direct way. You know it.

Bhante Vimalaraṁsi tells a story of a monk who is a famous monk in Burma. He is invited to a person's home for lunch and is offered the finest of curries and rice. The entire time the monk eats, he says "dukkha, dukkha," suffering, suffering.

He is trying to think his way to see the signs of existence, and that doesn't work. All it does it is to create an aversion to whatever you are labeling or noting *and* that's developing an unwholesome state, not insight at all.

This experience answers a lot of questions that you may have had brewing. Before this, everybody was talking about things happening so fast, but now your awareness is so sharp that you actually see each part of the experience. The twelve links of dependent origination are starting to come into focus, and you are beginning to see separate links. Moreover, you are beginning to see that they follow each other and that each link is dependent on the link before it.

After a while, it does appear this constant arising and passing away of consciousness does become tiresome. You wonder will it ever end? Is this all there is? It doesn't matter whether you're doing your walking meditation, or eating, or going to the toilet. You see all these consciousnesses continually. Is there a way out of this?

"As you instructed, I first radiated Joy in all directions, beginning with sending it out to individual directions five minutes each, then expanding the sublime joy outward. It grew larger and larger without stopping.

There was once again insight into the impermanence of "I" as it arose and passed away. The gaps in between each arising and passing away grew larger, and my focus shifted subtly to those blanks, where then the joy radiating in all directions was shifted to equanimity.

There was total disinterest in the impermanence of "I" and insight into the silliness of identifying a non-existent permanent I with every feeling, thought and action. Deeper experiential realization that feelings and thoughts were not under my control and that thoughts or mind objects in general were like what odors were to the nose, or sounds were to the ears. They came and went without me being involved. I continued to 6R nonetheless." S.D., California

—*Meditation Instruction:*

Small pinpoint lights may arise like little stars that twinkle and then fade away. These are the start of craving. They are indications of *taṇhā* just starting to arise. These are thoughts that are just starting to form. You feel a pull from those lights — a tightness. You realize that if you 6R them the moment they arise then thoughts don't arise; you see the relief in this. The 6Rs will return you to a state of balance and tranquility. Be sure to 6R them as soon as they arise.

These lights are "sticky" as they are little seeds of craving coming into existence. You now see the craving that exists in all thinking. And you see that is why constant thinking is so tiring and annoying to your mind.

Consider the other night when you couldn't get to sleep because you were thinking so much. It was suffering. Being successful with this meditation practice brings you the benefit of getting to sleep easily and having no bad dreams. This is one of the eleven benefits of Mettā meditation.

You might see illuminations expanding out like small suns; these are called *nimitta*. No, we are not talking about the nimitta or what some practices call *signs* that are used as focus points in concentration meditation, but these are merely forms and shapes that arise. This is the true meaning of nimitta. Let go of these and 6R them. You do not switch over and start focusing on them. They are just interesting phenomena that might distract you. Don't get involved with them.

If you were to take these lights as your meditation object, then that would be a concentration-absorption meditation practice, and that is *not* in the suttas. The Buddha had previously tried all these types of meditation, and he rejected that practice as leading to true awakening.

When you practice concentration with the breath meditation lights can arise, as well, and if you take these lights and concentrate on them, then, again, you are not practicing what is in the suttas. Please 6R them!

This is the influence of the commentaries like the Visuddhi Magga. The Visuddhi Magga has included many practices that are not in the suttas. This conflict should cause us to question which one is right.

In the base of infinite consciousness, some people have visions of Devas, Kuan Yin, Buddha, Jesus, or Mohammad; this is based on their belief systems. That all needs to be 6R'd so you can progress. If you feel very happy and joyful, sometimes there will be tears of joy. Allow the tears to come out; that is the sign of the *mudita* or joyful state in which you are abiding.

You may feel like things are slowing down — like watching a movie in slow motion; you may see each frame of consciousness arising and passing away, whether it is at the eye door or ear door. You may wobble and feel like you are woozy. Don't get attached to any of this; 6R all of it. None of these experiences are to be taken personally as me or mine; they should just be allowed. Your mindfulness is now getting very sharp, sharp enough to see individual consciousnesses.

—*Meditation Instruction:*

You will then be asked to start noticing the spaces between the consciousnesses. Try to become more aware of the silence *and* the tranquility that is there, and dwell in this quiet. Let everything else go. You will think "there is nothing." Patiently let this state deepen. This will lead you to the next base and the last of the Brahmavihāras. This is *Upekkhā* or Equanimity.

Sometimes around this level, the meditator may have the thought, "If I have no *self* then I should just die!" Fear can arise: "I have no control over anything; what can I do?" You just do what you always have — you *never had a self* in the first place, so nothing has changed. This is insight; it isn't suicidal thoughts by any means so don't worry.

The teacher will remind you that this is just your mind playing games; have a good laugh and lighten up. You won't die, not even close. Soon, you are moving into deeper, even more exciting territory.

"I was able to get more solidly into the realm of infinite consciousness in which I observed various things such as swirling colored geometric patterns interrupted by strobe lights. Sometimes I saw millions of tiny colored lights flashing randomly. The swirling patterns with strobe lights where the most common. I remembered you advised me to pay attention to the stillness between consciousnesses I looked between the strobes and 6Red. The colors came to a halt and disappeared, but I found if I looked closely there were subtle ripples in the black nothingness. I 6Red these and found the slowed or disappeared but never for long.

My mind was in an incredibly still state and yet I was not quite sure I was still in the meditative state. I reasoned that if I was still meditating that I should be able to return to radiating joy. So, I brought up joy and the colored patterns and strobe lights returned. Again, I 6Red that and returned to stillness." R.M., Japan

"There was once again insight into the impermanence of "I" as it arose and passed away. The gaps in between each arising and passing away grew larger, and my focus shifted subtly to those blanks, then the joy radiating in all directions was shifted to equanimity. S.D., California

Chapter Twelve: The Base of Nothing-ness — Equanimity

MN:111 section 15. "Again, monks, by completely surmounting the base of infinite consciousness, aware that 'there is nothing,' Sāriputta entered upon and abided in the base of nothingness.

Previously you saw the world existing as outside of yourself; now you see things as all in mind only. You still see different movements of mind, but they're not outside of mind. You have had a concept of yourself being in the world, which is constantly in the background of your thinking.

We all see ourselves in relationship to the world as a separate self or entity. Taking things personally, means we see ourselves doing things in our mind. We see ourselves having done things in the past. We see ourselves doing things now. And we see ourselves doing things in the future. "We" only exist in our minds. This idea or concept of "self" only exists in our mind, and now we see it.

Outside of the thinking mind, there is only seeing, hearing, touching, tasting, and smelling. Just sensations that are arising and passing away. Yet we identify these as having this self, this existence laid over the top of it — this "me" that is doing this, planning to do that, thinking about this, being a part of a team to create that. You are an actor in this dream of existence. It is all in your head. You are constantly creating this illusion of self, moment to moment. They are just images.

Now you finally start to come out of the dream and only see what is there. Gross thinking stops. Conceptual engagement stops. Now in the seeing, there is only seeing, in the hearing only hearing, etc. Nothing happens in the past, and nothing happens in the future — it is all happening now. And in this clear present, there is no self. There is only awareness of what happens at the sense doors moment to moment. It becomes very quiet—you have never experienced this before. This is the awareness and experience of the base of nothingness.

This jhāna is like the part in the Matrix movie where Keanu Reeves wakes up from his dream existence in this machine-created mental world and realizes that he is in a pod just dreaming his life experience. Like him, we are waking out of our dream of self to find nothing but an impersonal process — a never-ending stream of events.

Now it's like your consciousness stops paying attention to general body awareness and sensations and jumps up into your head. You are no longer paying attention to the awareness that has anything to do with the body. You see everything as happening from mind, and physically from the head area.

You are only attentive to mind. Concepts stop. Thoughts are now just observing thoughts and not being taken personally. They are not defining your world anymore. In fact, most thoughts simply stop.

Since concepts come from thoughts, and things come from concepts, then the lack of things leads us to the realm of *No-thing-ness!* You are now seeing clearly - without the noise and without creating stories about everything.

Some people will say it even feels like being in the desert all alone — in total desolation. There is nothing around but sand…it is pleasant, yet different from anything you have ever felt.

You start to understand the links of dependent origination called Nāma-Rūpa or Mentality/Materiality (Name and Form). There is mind that is dependent upon the body. Both are distinct, yet work together. One cannot be without the other. But now you see, with direct insight, that there is the body itself separate from mind.

For example, there is the breath going in and out, and then the mentality or mind which is made up of feeling, perception, and consciousness. There is the physical breath, and there is the knowing — the perception of the breath and knowing what it is doing and how it feels. This is the Mentality/Materiality link of dependent origination.

With the dropping of the concept of things out there and of your perceived feeling of your separate existence in the world, your awareness pulls in. The ever-present, worrying "dream" of you disappears. No more thoughts that carry you away into the future or the past. No more thoughts are creating this or that world. You just exist in the present. Your awareness is clear and free of your conceptual self-image.

Without these concepts, there is only the present, the arising and passing away of feeling and sensations. This is all that you see. No past or future lives now. This is mind's attention without craving embedded in it, without the overlaying of the idea of self or soul.

In this silence of nothingness, you start to see much more subtle phenomena that were hidden by our noisy minds. Very interesting things are here. There is definitely not nothing!

MN:111 section 16. "And the states in the base of nothingness..."

Before, in the second arūpa jhāna if infinite consciousness, you were radiating Joy in all six directions. Where you were feeling joy before, now you're feeling equanimity that is very, very strong, and you have this very fine balance of mind. Now you take this equanimity as your object and radiate it to all beings in all directions. This particular level of mind is by far one of the more fascinating states that are experienced in meditation. Now there is no sadness nor happiness, just balance. When asked how you feel, you will always report that you are fine. "Everything is fine." "I have nothing to say." Just fine.

From an Online Retreat Report:

"Sitting #1 (1 hour): Joy for 19 minutes. I saw patterns and glowing balls. I 6Rd these. Then went into equanimity. I saw golden stupas; Buddha statues and a celestial being emitting a brilliant

light. I 6R'd these as they came up. Next 30 minutes was with sending equanimity in all directions with golden light emitting from my crown. I 6r'd whatever came up. 15 minutes was the best with keeping my mind on the object of my meditation." C.B. Sri Lanka

<u>*From an Online Retreat Report:*</u>

After about 10 minutes, I could feel myself going deeper before the descent stopped. After 5 minutes or so at that level, I started to descend again to the next "level". My notes record "got deeper in plateau - like steps" and that was what it was like. I must have gone down in 3 or 4 "steps", spending 5 minutes or so before moving down to the next plateau. At one plateau I recall seeing a vista like a black, clear night-sky with thousands of tiny pin-pricks of light twinkling away. On the next level down, I saw what I can only describe as a really big area covered with rows and rows of ball-shaped translucent shapes, the skirts of which were gently rippling. I described them as "jellyfish" because of their translucent nature. The odd ball/jellyfish would occasionally speed off away from this vista.

"But mainly, the visual field was still, and quiet. After the "jellyfish", the next descent was longer, at the bottom of which the blackness was unmoving, absolutely still. I can remember wondering whether I was dead! Whether I was or wasn't was of no interest; the possibility certainly didn't upset me. Around this point at the "deepest level (I didn't move down from this level), what I describe as "tingles" moved throughout the body in waves. After a couple of passes, this stopped and the absolute still quiet remained. At this point of the sit, the quiet was quite "solid". Not the quiet when you turn off a radio and think "that's quiet", but rather a quiet where there's absolutely no point from which any noise could originate. An absence of anything that could disturb. A quiet/stillness that is not capable of being broken." L.M., Australia

Others feel the tranquility coming from you. There seems to be a glow in your face: a radiance. Any stress lines have all but disappeared.

If you do not put quite enough energy into watching that equanimity, your mind gets dull. You don't have sleepiness, but a dullness can occur. If you put in a little bit too much energy, your mind gets restless. Now you must steady your energy. This is where you are balancing the seven factors of awakening. We will go through these later.

If restlessness arises because you put in too much energy, you are no longer in the jhāna. You're caught by a hindrance. And because of the way the hindrances work, they don't just come one at a time. For example, when you have restlessness, it's not just restlessness; it's the restlessness, as well as the dislike of the restlessness. So, you have two hindrances that you get to work with; hindrances pile up on top of hindrances!

It's quite easy to let restlessness go and balance your energy by this time if you are patient. It's like walking the finest tightrope you've ever seen; like walking on a spider web — it's that fine. Being in that kind of balance, it just takes a little "tweak" — a little "twerp" — and "whoop," you could be knocked off balance. And then you should work with it again, bring in a little more energy, some more mindfulness. If this is too much, back off again. This is where working with the energy is incredibly interesting and subtle.

The most important thing here is using your Mindfulness to observe what is there in mind and to balance it by backing off or adding energy to your practice. By observing these states, you will affect them naturally — therefore Mindfulness is the most important factor of awakening. The Investigation Factor arises when mind's movement is clearly seen. Investigation balances both energy and lack of energy automatically by seeing what is out of balance and changing it.

In quantum physics, it is posited that you can change a process by observing it; this is what mindfulness does. Mind observes itself, and change takes place.

Sometimes you may not make progress because something is nagging at the back of your mind. It is a subtle desire that you are identifying with — you are looking for something to happen — perhaps wanting Nibbāna to come and looking for it by thinking about it. It should be 6R'd. It can be a pesky desire, but eventually, you will get tired of it. Nibbāna will never happen if there is this craving there. Nibbāna will happen when mind loses all its craving and movement.

Again, you may have fear arise and think that you don't exist! As before, you should just 6R that fear and continue. It will disappear soon enough. That is just more craving.

MN:111 section 16. "And the states in the base of nothingness — the perception of the base of nothingness and the unification of mind; the contact, feeling, perception, volition, and mind..."

Equanimity gets very deep here, and this should be your object of meditation now. You should imagine yourself surrounded and enveloped by the feeling of equanimity. You should radiate this feeling outward from your whole mind. Keep a small smile going, as this will warn you of unwholesome states coming in.

Like a candle emits heat and light, you simply sit and let the equanimity radiate out by itself. You almost see it go out. If there is stress from sending out the feeling, then you are pushing too hard. You should just let it seep out like a fog but point it to the direction in which you intend it to go. If there is tension, then just 6R it. Do not push the feeling of equanimity out. Pushing it will create more tension. That is trying to control feeling with your thoughts. It doesn't work.

A lighthouse emits light in all directions. It doesn't push anything; the light just shines outward. All you do is switch on the light.

If you are distracted by a sound or a touch, then 6R it and come back to radiating the feeling, but only 6R if it draws your attention away from the feeling. If you see small movements, or there are wispy thoughts in the background, yet you are still aware of and collected on your meditation object, radiating equanimity in the six directions, ignore those small distractions. That is just noise. Don't 6R unless your attention is drawn away.

—*Meditation Instruction:*

Now you are starting your sitting using the feeling equanimity as your object. You radiate the feeling of equanimity each of the six directions for five minutes each and then to all directions at the same time for the rest of the sitting. When you do the walking meditation, you radiate equanimity to all directions at the same time and 6R any distractions.

Sit longer now: one hour, one and a half hours, two hours, three hours. If you feel like you want to get up, then sit another five minutes and see if that urge goes away.

Mental activity gets quieter and quieter. Just observe what is there at the moment. Mind will feel bright and energetic, with little movement. You will start to see the link of *consciousness* arising and passing away. This is a potential. You will see this start of the movement, and then it blossoms into your awareness as something, be it seeing, hearing, or a tangible feeling. It is like you know that you are going to see something, and then you do. Gradually you will see all the processes in the links of dependent origination that occur before contact.

You perceive that everything you experience takes place within your mind only. What makes up the real "you" is mind and mind objects coming and going. Do you really have a body, or do you just see this image and call it a body? Are "you" hearing a sound, or is it only sound consciousness arising and a perception of "you" "hearing" it?

What is consciousness? You see now that consciousness knows itself. You stop identifying with it as you. It reflects the *form* that is in front of it — like seeing a red rose in a mirror. Bhikkhu Ñāṇananda,[xii] the author of *Concept and Reality*, calls it a hall of mirrors in which the mirror itself is self-aware at that moment with whatever sight or sound form is cognized. There is nobody in the room itself, but it is the mirrors themselves that are "aware of being aware." The mind overlays a concept of self, but there are only the mirrors and the reflections.

The consciousness arises, and then it is gone. There was nothing before it and nothing after it. There was never anyone in the hall except the mirrors. You just thought there was.

You now see what is there directly without concepts. You see that consciousness only experiences itself with no experiencer. The concept of self is not there anymore. There are thousands of moments that make up each event of hearing or seeing. "You" exist for that moment only. Then there is another moment, and "you" hear again. There is a space between these moments where there is *nothing*. Now you are perceiving the silence and the arising and passing away of objects in that silence.

If the sound had not arisen, then "you" would not have arisen. You would not have been born into conscious awareness had there been no sound as a condition. That is rebirth moment to moment right there. And since there is nothing between the consciousnesses, how can there be an idea of an all-pervading soul or self? You live for a moment and then die. *Physical* death is just one moment from this body to another. You really die every moment; your body dying has nothing to do with *you* dying.

—Meditation Instruction:

When things get quiet, you might try to add something, adjust something, or try to watch something. Since "nothing" is arising, you might get a little bored. In this case, notice the craving mind wanting to make something happen, wanting to control. 6R *that* mind right there and let it go, then just be there with no movement. 6R the concept of a *controller*. Just be in the feeling of Equanimity as it radiates. Do not move in mind at all. Like the Beatles song, "Let it be, let it be."

Distractions that Arise — How to Adjust

- Too much energy, you become restless — you need to reduce your energy. Take tranquility as your object of meditation. This will bring in calm. 6R your desire to control the process. Add it to the feeling of equanimity.

- Not enough energy, you become sleepy or dull — you need to add more effort and increase your curiosity about what is happening. Take more interest. You can also get up and walk to arouse energy. Do some fast walking. Find some stairs to go up and down. The longer you sit, the more you should walk. Many meditators avoid the walking but then wonder why they doze off or zone out when they sit for long periods. You need to keep your blood moving and your energy up.

The Buddha and his monks walked everywhere they went and thus kept their bodies very healthy. Alms rounds could be very long and strenuous, but it would pay off in energy for the meditation.

6R any boredom (a subtle aversion reaction) and get through it. At times, very little happens, and you must be very gentle and patient. Then you will go deeper. U Sīlananda, one of Bhante's teachers, would always tell him: "Patience leads to Nibbāna."

There are seven awakening factors at work. These factors need to be adjusted. Don't worry too much about doing the balancing at this point. Just let the mindfulness do its job. Some meditators will control too much and try to make their mind calm with whatever factor they think they need. But too much of this will lead to restlessness. You must balance the *desire* to balance by backing off and letting things get into balance by themselves.

Venerable Bhante Vimalaraṁsi often reminds his advanced students to remember that their job as a meditator is to simply observe how mind's attention moves from one thing to another. Mindfulness is not about controlling any movements. One of the most difficult things to do is to just observe without trying to control anything.

Seven Factors of Awakening:

1. *Sati — Mindfulness*

2. *Dhammavicaya — Investigation of experience*

3. *Viriya — Energy*

4. *Pīti — Joy*

5. *Passaddhi — Tranquility; Relaxed in mind*

6. *Samādhi — Collectedness of mind*

7. *Upekkhā — Equanimity*

Some people may complain about distractions happening in their body. They can feel pain somewhere in their body. This is not real pain but a really subtle hindrance coming up in their mind. Do not pay any attention to your body anymore.

Most pain will now be what is known as "meditation pain." This is different from a real pain. An actual pain comes because you are sitting too long or sitting twisted in a weird way and you are hurting your body.

This meditation pain is the pain of the hindrances coming up. It mostly is the pain of restlessness. Restlessness is a painful feeling, but it is in your mind, and you must determine to not be moved by it but soften into it, let it be and relax the tension and tightness that is there.

You are only concerned with mind now. You should sit for long periods of time. Sit one hour, two hours, and even three and four hours. The longer you sit, the more time mind has to calm down. So far the record for Bhante's students is two days in one sitting completed by a man in Indonesia and recently a man in the USA! And that really paid off — the results were phenomenal. And he just got up and walked away with no pain or stiffness; he felt just fine.

Eventually, mind will become very calm, and equanimity will become very profound. We then come to the next arūpa jhāna where we leave all the brahmavihāras behind.

Chapter Thirteen: The Base of Neither Perception-Nor Non-Perception

MN:111 section 17. "Again, bhikkhus, by completely surmounting the base of nothingness, Sāriputta entered upon and abided in the base of neither-perception-nor-non-perception.

Now you will not be able to radiate the feeling of equanimity anymore — it will just naturally stop. It just isn't there anymore, and if you try to radiate it, then that will cause some tension to arise. If you notice this happening, then just sit in the silence and observe. If you are unsure, then try radiating equanimity again, and if it comes up then continue it once again until it finally fades on its own. If you bring up the feeling and now it causes a slight tension (in your head), even radiating that feeling, then you can stop and just be in this quiet mind.

—Meditation Instruction:

You should now take **Clear Quiet Mind** as your object of meditation. Notice the stillness and the tranquil feeling that is there. Let yourself sink into that. Now the instructions will change a little. 6R any movements or vibrations as soon as they start to arise, and then go back to a clear, quiet state of mind. You take this empty silence as the object of meditation and watch for any movements arising. 6R as soon as they arise and relax the tension out of any of the movements and come back to just this quiet and peaceful state. You might see a flicker or a light or some movement there. 6R that as soon as they arise.

Soon the this exquisite stillness becomes your object. Before in earlier sittings, mind was expanding, now it becomes so still and subtle that it is hard to tell whether anything arises or not. Your mindfulness now has come to a level where there is nothing that escapes your 6R tool. You have a sense of power over the arising phenomena that you have never felt before. By allowing things to arise and relax into them you actually, in a way, have achieved control over them…

No More Feeling

You now have come to the end of the meditation of the Brahmavihāras, which has the four Divine Abodes as its objects. You started with the meditation object of Mettā, or loving-kindness, progressed automatically to Karuṇā, or Compassion, and then to Mud;tā, or Joy, and this finally transformed into Upekkhā or deep equanimity. Now even that is gone. You begin the next phase of the meditation: just observation of movements within mind.

As the feeling of equanimity which brought you to this point fades away, you are now going to be mindful of mind and mind-objects. You will start to observe what is there, and subsequently, see very small movements arise. As soon as you see any movement or vibration, you need to relax. Your mind will become very, very still for long periods of time. This deep quietness of mind and lack of any distractions at all can last for twenty minutes or thirty minutes, and even for an hour. This exquisite silence is where mind is absolutely pure! The longer you can sit with this still mind, the better.

From an Online Retreater: Sitting #3

"I went straight into equanimity. I saw some images initially. 6R'd these as they came up. I radiated equanimity from my crown.

I 6R'd whatever came up. It felt like things were coming up fast! I felt a little restless because of this. Eventually, the equanimity stopped radiating. What I noticed was golden energy from the base of my spine rose up to my crown.

Golden light all around. Eventually, it dissipated after some time. I was in quietness for around 20 minutes. The time felt like 8pm as it was very quiet even from my noisy surroundings. We live in Colombo near a noisy main road. Lots of horns etc... But it felt like 8pm when there is little traffic and noise." C.B. Sri Lanka

Gradually the Nothingness jhāna gives way to the Realm of Neither-Perception-nor-Non-Perception — the fourth arūpa jhāna. Mind is so subtle at this point that the only way you know that you've experienced that state is that when you come out, you can reflect on what you saw there. Some feeling was still there, although it's subtle, and perception is kind of there and kind of not.

Now your instructions are to simply observe mind objects that are arising and passing away in this bright clear mind. You don't want to start this observation before the time is right. You began your sitting by radiating the feeling of equanimity to each direction. However, you may not be able to.

If you try to generate any feeling at all, it may cause tension in your mind. Never create tension where there was none before. If you have doubt, then you can try generating a feeling of stillness to see if stillness comes up and will flow out on its own. This stillness can be likened to looking up into the night sky — so tranquil and still. If you feel like you are forcing it, then just stop. This means now that it is time just to observe. If, on the other hand, you can radiate then just continue doing that until it stops again.

As you watch mind and 6R any movements or vibrations that start to arise, all activity will slow down. Mind's activity will almost flatten out to nothing at all. There are things in mind, but they are no longer pulling at your conscious awareness. An obstacle here can be a tendency to get involved in everything that arises and analyze where it came from. Why did it arise? Where did it come from? These questions are not valid here. That is just more thinking, a sort of restlessness to do something.

Let all the analyzing go. The analyzing is for the therapists and psychologists and is not a part of the Buddha's path. There is no end to it anyway. There is an endless amount of stuff coming and going, and you can never analyze it all. One of Venerable Bhante Vimalaraṁsi's teachers, The Most Venerable Sayadaw U Paṇḍita, told him that analyzing things is a Western disease!

One meditator reported that past lives would arise as little bubbles. He would go off and investigate them to see what was there. In the end, this was harmful to his practice, and he was letting craving get the better of him. It took many years for him to get tired of this and finally 6R these memory bubbles dispassionately.

Psychologists will want to look at where these thoughts come from, but we don't. We are just observing the process and how it arises.

If you look at it this way, when you start meditating your mind has big jerky kinds of movements. As you get deeper into your meditation, the movements become less and less. When you get into the arūpa jhānas, the movements start turning into just vibrations. As you go higher into the arūpa jhānas, the vibrations become faster and finer. When you get to the state of neither-perception-nor-non-perception, there are only slight movements that are very subtle; it is hard to tell if they are there or not.

Your awareness will start to go inward, or some say mind appears to grow smaller. Mind is there, but it is hard to perceive. It is like a jigsaw puzzle that is now starting to lose pieces. Gradually, there is only just a glimmering of what was there. So few objects are arising now that it appears there is less and less of you there at all.

This is the time when you want to make sure that you have developed that habit of relaxing continually, all the time. That way, when you get into this state, you're doing this as an automatic habit.

—*Meditation Instruction:*

The only way you know that you've experienced this very subtle state is by reflecting afterward what happened while you were in that state. When you come out, take a few minutes for reflection, and 6R anything that arises. Don't get into stories about it, just reflect and let go. Since you haven't experienced this before, your mind will naturally think about what happened. Just 6R those thoughts. Don't stop them. Just let them be and fade away. Relax into them.

What is this relaxing doing? When you relax, the movement of mind becomes less and less until you finally get to a state in which you cannot see any gross movement, but there is still a little bit of vibration. The more you relax, the more the vibration slows down, because it is the craving that is creating the movement. Relaxing removes the craving, and mind settles further. You still have those small movements even when you get into neither-perception-nor-non-perception.

If you are working with a teacher, you will likely be asked, "Were you in a state that is like you were asleep but you were awake?" Movement of mind slows to smaller and smaller activities. You start having gaps in your awareness. There is no longer a fully consistent conscious awareness. Mind slows, like ice freezing.

There are levels of Neither-Perception. At first, mind may slow down, like you are in a dream. There might be a story going on, yet, like a dream, when you come out of that state, it makes no sense — though it did make sense when you were experiencing it. For example, it might have made sense if a bird was talking and you were completely fine with that in the dream but when you come out of this state you wonder why you thought birds could talk!

In this state, there can be images that arise, colors, shapes, patterns. You should 6R all of those if you are aware enough at that moment. But at times, your awareness just isn't strong enough to notice them. It's like telling someone to be mindful in a dream. Later, in or after your sitting, if you start to reflect on what happened you can 6R at that time.

Still, your mindfulness gets progressively sharper as you go in and out of this deeper level and, eventually, all of the dreamy images or patterns just disappear. There is barely anything left at all. There might even just be what appears to be a blank screen — just blackness — but you knew you were there when you came out. Nothing actually stopped since you were aware of time passing during that state.

Be aware that during your sitting, generally, you may go into a dreamy state and, since you have heard that the base of neither-perception-nor-non-perception is a dreamlike space, you may wonder whether you are experiencing this jhāna. Actually, this may only be sloth and torpor, which needs to be 6R'd. Here you have confused the state of dullness with the deeper state of the arūpa jhāna.

This vague torpor-like state can be completely blank. This is very definitely a low-energy, low-mindfulness state. When you "wake up" out of this state, it's more like waking up out of sleep — there will be some energy, but it is weak and doesn't last. Or you just may be drowsy. You might think this low-energy state is special, but it's just an absence of awareness.

The difference between these states is that when you go into the neither-perception state, it will be from a bright and energetic, clear space. You will be very mindful and alert.

It might be confusing to you later but going from a low energy, dull state into a faraway torpor state is not the way to go deeper. Be watchful and question yourself about this. You may be overestimating your level of awareness when it is just a torpor state. If so, then you need to build up your mindfulness and use your 6Rs more. When you go into the fourth arūpa jhāna, your energy will be very high, but the tranquility and stillness will be even stronger.

You can be guaranteed that coming out of this deeper state you will not be sleepy — you will have more energy than ever before. If you do feel low energy, then it is time to get up and do some brisk walking to get the body energy restored.

As you sit more and for longer, you may go into neither-perception several times in a sitting, and each time you will go deeper than before. When you come out of this state, please don't get up from your session. Just continue and 6R any disturbances that show up. Keep sitting. 6R whatever you remember that happened in that state. Your mind will be more active and full of energy coming out, but you should just let it settle back. Each time you go into the jhāna, it will be deeper than the last.

MN:111 section 18. "He emerged mindful from that attainment. Having done so, he contemplated the states that had passed, ceased, and changed, thus..."

When you sit for long periods in deeper meditation, you will get into this neither-perception-nor-non-perception state.

You will feel very silent in mind and energized. There won't be much movement of mind here at all.

When you are at this level in your meditation, and you have your noonday meal (lunch), you will not get drowsy. Just a slight heaviness that passes or even nothing at all, so strong now mind has become. You may sleep less and wake up often at night. If you do wake up, then you can try doing a sitting for as long as you can, and then go back to sleep when you get tired. This works for some people but not for others, it interrupts the sleep cycle and the rest of the next day is sleepy and dull. Be attentive and see what works for you.

Around this time some meditators on retreat may want to get up earlier – like 2–3 a.m. — and sit longer in the morning. The teacher will encourage you to sit longer. You can ask the teacher to allow you to sit through the lunch period. Food can be put aside for you to have later. Thus, it is called the noonday meal. It is a meal around noon, meaning it can be pushed out to 1 p.m. or perhaps 2 p.m. or further — but it still is your only substantial meal of the day. Monks must eat starting at 11 a.m. and finish by 12 p.m., but it's okay for lay-people to bend this rule.

You are now at a point in your meditation practice where backing away from any movement in mind is what your meditation has become. Seeing states arising impersonally is important. Reacting now to states with more dispassion, and just observing, without any real interest loosens your attachment to them. It is all just stuff — nothing to be followed or investigated.

Let's review here our preliminary methods and goal for our practice. We are using samatha meditation as the means to tranquilize and calm the mind; like spreading oil on water. This is by using a variety of different feelings — the mettā, the compassion, joy, and equanimity that arise one by one when we start with mettā. This is the Brahmvihāra practice.

We are observing states arising in the jhānas as they arise one by one — be they wholesome or unwholesome and seeing their impermanent, soulless nature. The samatha part of this process calms down the noise so that we can observe much closer the arising phenomena. This is the insight part or vipassanā. So this is samatha-vipassanā, both working together.

So now what happens is that gradually movement slows down to the point where we are no longer "drowning" in thoughts and distractions and can now let go of the brahmavihāras as our meditation object — in fact, they just fade away. Now we are observing movements against our clear, quiet mind as our meditation object. We are clear and balanced enough not to be swayed by the now small distractions and vibrations.

Gradually even these small movements will stop, and all mental activity will stop. The pond of our mind will not have one single ripple there. All of a sudden awareness and consciousness will *stop* for a moment. There will be super clarity right after this as now see deeper than we have ever seen before. We see the deepest aspect of the mental process. So, this is where we are headed. Let's keep going.

There is this small "wrapper" of craving around each state that arises. It is what you think of as "you." It will take the feeling that is arising as "my feeling," and there are a tiny story and perception about what that is. When anything arises, your mind instantly perceives that object is being observed by a "you." There is the object, and the self perceiving the object. This is craving — it is this sense you have of "you."

Actually, there is no you there at all. There is the object, there is the sense base, and there is consciousness; that is, the visual object, the eye organ itself, and the eye consciousness.

Mind interprets these processes arising and passing away as part of a permanent "you." But what is really happening is that feeling arises, and there is this sense of a "you" feeling it. There is consciousness, but there is mistakenly the perception that this little "you" is a self that is feeling it. Some people even see this little image of themselves and the deluded mind identifies that as the real "you." But it is only a picture — you aren't there at all. Self is only a concept.

Think about this for a moment. At night you have dreams, and you definitely feel like you exist in these dream phantasies. You are doing this and that and are reacting with horror or pleasure, depending on the situation. Isn't this just like your life. You know you don't really exist in the dream, but when you are awake you think you exist and react just like when you are dreaming! Isn't this the same? In fact, the Buddha realized that the concept of self was false and this is why we say the Buddha awakened — out of this dream of self.

Also, by personalizing each arising feeling, by making each object arising "yours," you could tend to think that you made the experience happen. This is very important to notice. This is the delusion of a "self" controlling every arising state. You will feel that "I made this come into being" or "I control this or that state that has arisen."

The fact is that you do not control anything. The deep insight of dependent origination is that everything arises from a cause without there being any self doing it or making it happen or controlling it. You have nothing to say about it. With a deep understanding of this, you will feel *relief* because you no longer have this self-imposed burden of thinking *you control* every mental state. What a relief to not feel responsible for every thought! You didn't think them — they alone are responsible for "their" existence.

When something in mind arises, whether it is an image, light, or thought, just back away very, very gently. See the state rise into existence from nowhere. It does not matter why it came up. It just did, and you didn't make it happen. It arose based on conditions. No king is commanding this to arise and that to arise. There is no controller, nobody in charge.

You might be watching with too much energy and bear down on objects coming and going. Lighten up and come to a quiet, still point where your awareness, is very still. There are simply vibrations that arise and pass away.

Don't think you are controlling anything. If you were controlling things, you could determine when you would be happy or sad, and you know you can't do that. In fact, try to use your investigation to peer very closely into that force, that urge, that wants to control. It is constantly there in the background with each arising of feeling. A subtle "you" arises that likes the feeling or doesn't. That is the craving or sense of a controller — the false belief in a personal self. So, the moment that feeling or even a little image of "you" arises relax and 6R it. Don't lean into it. Release and back away. Let the feeling fade, leaving only stillness and where there is nothing except observation.

The sutta talks about the factor of *decision*. Did you know that when you "make a decision," it is yet another constituent of mind that just arises that has no controller behind it? When you see this factor arise in your meditation try 6'ring it and you are left just sitting there — no action occurs since you let go of the decision.

If you somehow think you will go to sit, and then you continue to think about which pillow to use, you might see the precise deciding moment from where you "decide" which pillow to use. There is a moment in which your "decision" arises. If you back away and gently just allow everything to arise but very carefully watch it with your investigation factor, you will see the decision factor arise entirely on its own. And it also then passes away. There appears a call to action that arises from the craving embedded in it. This craving is the push you feel to go into action.

You are now unperturbed and content just to let go of anything arising. It's not yours. It's just stuff. You see this with a mind that is purified from craving — not taking things personally. This is seeing things with the "eye of wisdom," seeing things as they really are. And it feels very good! Finally, you come to an unparalleled level of balance called disenchantment, followed by an even deeper state of dispassion, which will open the door to the "unconditioned."

The more time you spend in Neither-Perception-nor-Non-Perception, the more mind is purified. Bhante says that much merit is made in this state. Merit is like a store of wholesome action leading to very good future results. This is like your karmic bank account. Developing a purer and purer mind will help you advance toward the attainment.

As you continue to sit in this state movements of mind's attention, have virtually stopped as craving recedes. This is now the time to be patient and persevere. Continue to observe and 6R, relaxing into any movement or flickering of mind.

If a sound arises and your attention starts to move there, immediately back away from it, relax, and come back to a bright clear mind. If there is any interest in the sound, you need to 6R the desire to see what it is. Any desire to do anything at all is to be 6R'd.

You will get to the point where you feel like your awareness has stopped. You are just sitting quietly, not caught up in the mindstream which is constantly rushing forward. The Buddha talks about it as stopping in a river with the water now seen going by you yet you now have become an immovable rock. The sense of "you" isn't moving anymore, it has become detached from the stream of events, and there is a sublime relief in this.

Any movement you now observe as a disturbance to your stillness. You notice that movement is suffering, dukkha. There might be a desire to push away any slight movements but 6R that aversion and let it be. You can't push away anything. Remember, you have no control over anything. All you can do is observe and 6R.

Any desire to analyze what is happening or what is arising should not be followed. We are only interested in the process — the arising and passing away. Questions about why things come up can never be fully resolved. The reason may not even come from this lifetime, so you can never really know what might be the cause of a hindrance. You don't need to understand where things come from; we leave that to the psychologist; we just 6R it and let it go.

Hindrances are karmically produced by unwholesome actions; that is, the previous breaking of precepts — whether in this life or others. All we can do is stop breaking precepts now and 6R any disturbance that arises from when we broke them in the past.

When you see a sight, based on that contact a feeling arises — pleasant, unpleasant, or neither pleasant nor unpleasant (neutral). Immediately, upon the feeling arising, there is craving: wanting to enjoy what it is or to push it away.

You understand as soon as you see something, that very seeing process has craving in it. 6R and relax into that seeing process as soon as it catches your awareness. Notice there is a very subtle tension as soon as your eye locks onto the sight — that is what "pulls" your attention to see it. The moment your mind turns to observing anything at all, you should be relaxing into it right there. Do not let the craving gain a foothold on your attention. Let it go. In most circumstances craving is not that strong but, as Bhante Vimalaraṁsi says, it is definitely persistent.

Actually, there is no such thing as "mind pulling your attention." The sound arises, and the craving arises. It seems like some sort of "you" is being pulled to the sound, but that's not what is happening. Sound and craving arise together, giving the illusion that somebody is being pulled to it. That is the delusion of the personal you. In fact, the sight or taste or whatever arises has the craving "embedded" in it and the "you" that arises is right there in that sensation.

You don't exist anywhere else at that moment other than in hearing the sound. Why do you arise at that moment? You arise because you wanted to hear it.

You (your so-called permanent self) is actually being born into existence at that moment of identification. Before that, there was just the fading of the last consciousness arising. Then the new sound vibration arose, which triggered the craving to arise, and the personal "you" was created once more. This is the process of dependent origination — causes and conditions are constantly arising and passing away. Perhaps we can say you were "re-born again" ...and again, and again.

The Nature of Consciousness

The five aggregates all arise in each moment, but they are affected by craving and clinging. This is due to their being taken personally. In fact, the aggregates all arise at the same time, creating your world at that moment. Then they pass away. You only exist in each arising moment, and then you are gone — completely — until the next contact and feeling arise. And this all happens thousands of times in the blink of an eye, which is why we appear to "feel" like a continuous entity with no breaks. You had already seen this phenomenon occur when you were in the second arūpa jhāna — the realm of infinite consciousness.

Then, based on some outside cause, you are born yet again to hear, see, or touch. If not for that vibration or contact at the sense door, you would simply not come into existence at all. You don't exist outside of that sense contact which sparks you into existence! This is quite an insight when it arises. There is no underlying Self that experiences the sense bases. The senses only experience themselves.

"You" do not die when your body dies — you are actually "dying" every moment and then coming back into existence only to disappear again. Consciousness is like the bubbles generated from a quickly flowing stream. The water hits the rocks like the sense objects hit the sense doors. The mist that arises as the water splashes over the rocks is like eye forms (sights) colliding with the eye sense organ, creating the drops or "mist" of consciousness.

This is your awareness arising and passing away dependent on the sixfold sense base, which is your body. This awareness seems real and feels like a permanent self at that moment, but then in the next moment, the bubble of awareness pops and disappears. Birth, death, birth, death, millions of times in a single second.

From a scientific viewpoint, these are just neurons firing in the brain and can be explained, but we see for ourselves through meditation, through direct knowledge, how this happens in mind. Then we can know the truly impersonal nature of the process, the truly scientific view of impersonality.

Science already says there is no self; there are only bodily and mental elements and nothing else. But other scientists still argue that there must be a deeper self or soul that does exist — it is just beyond what they can measure. Real insight into the psychophysical process is defined by actually believing the data you observe. In other words, researchers say there are only neurons firing inside a mass of gray matter, and thus there can be no real soul there. Yet, these scientists don't even believe their own data and still think there is an underlying soul present. Habitual opinions run deep.

We will see that the actual fuel behind the mental movement is craving. There is a bodily process going on and a mental one. The bodily parts of this process are the *chemicals* in the brain reacting together — this is the body. The *result* of the chemical reaction is consciousness which is mind-body, and mind.

Arising from where? We don't know while we are observing it, but the Buddha does explain this. It's about karma and its results — the residue of past unwholesome or wholesome actions which was caused by the breaking or keeping the precepts. The mental process just arises from conditions that are there. This is seen by direct knowledge.

Through an experiential understanding of these insights, mind itself is *changed*. Understanding is the reason. Craving ceases, some neurons don't fire, and "you" (craving) doesn't come into being.

You hear that your favorite uncle has died. Previously you would have been distraught, but now, because you see the true nature of things, you start to understand that everything does die — and that's ok. It isn't unexpected; it is part of life.

Neuroscientists can observe how the brain works, but only understanding attained by direct experience can fundamentally change the conditioned reaction in the brain.

It is doubtful that observing electrical readouts on a *f*MRI monitor (*functional* MRI – measures blood and oxygen levels in the brain) will ever lead to awakening. Why? Because only direct experience can give us deep insight into how things really work.

The Buddha said: "All mental phenomena have mind as their forerunner..."[xiii] Thus, we must look at mind first and see this clearly; then we will understand the interplay between mind and body. When we see this properly, we see the impersonal aspect of the process at that time. Delusion is eliminated because we understand that there was never anyone there in the first place to experience the "I like it" or "I don't like it" mind. This is what delusion means. We know that self is only a concept. And it is the supreme *concept*!

Listing of the Jhānas and the Meditation Object

First Jhāna	Loving-Kindness (Mettā)
Second Jhāna	Loving-Kindness (Mettā)
Third Jhāna	Loving-Kindness (Mettā)
Fourth Jhāna	Loving-Kindness (Mettā)
Base of Infinite Space	Compassion (Karuṇā)
Base of Infinite Consciousness	Joy (Muditā)
Base of Nothingness	Equanimity (Upekkhā)
Base of Neither-Perception-nor-Non-Perception	Clear, Quiet Mind

Chart of Jhānas & Characteristics

No.	Jhana	Characteristics	Meditative Progress	Time on Object	Avg Sitting Time
0	Worldly- None	Wandering Mind	Unable to stay on object	5 Sec - 2 min.	30min or less
1	1st Jhana	Joy, Excitement, Happiness, Tranquility	Only wholesome observation thoughts	3-5 min.	30min-45min
2	2nd Jhana	Bigger but more subtle Joy. Confidence, floating feeling	Verbalizing causes tension in head.	3-6 min.	45min-60min
3	3rd Jhana	Joy turns to contentment and happiness. Increasing equanimity.	Lose bodily feeling. "My hands are missing!"	3-10 min.	45min-60min
4	4th Jhana	Equanimity – happy feeling fades - just balance remains	Feeling of loving-kindness rises to the head.	5-10 min.	60min-1.25 hrs
5	Base of Infinite Space	Mind starts to expand outward	Lovingkindness now turns to Compassion	5-10 min.	1 hr. to 1.5 hrs
6	Base of Infinite Consciousness	See moments of consciousness arise. Seeing Impersonality	Feeling of Compassion turns to Joy	10-15 min.	1 hr. to 1.5 hrs
7	Base of Nothingness	Awareness in head. Lights, flickers – no thoughts at all	Feeling of Joy turns to Feeling of Equanimity	15-30 min.	1.5 to 2 hrs
8	Base of Neither Perceptions nor Non- Perception	Subtle vibrations, dreamy, No thoughts at all for long periods	The feeling of Equanimity just stops-Observe Quiet Mind Object	20-60 min.	1.5 to 3 hrs
	Cessation	No perception feeling or consciousness - like a light switch turning off.	A "space" or blackout in the mental stream.		
	Nibbana	Seeing links, moment of relief, then joy.	Perceive world differently -bright colors etc.		

Chapter Fourteen: The Door to Nibbāna

As you continue sitting, there will be the experience of strong stillness and balance happening, and you will be able to sit for long periods of time without many distractions arising. The mental activity is very quiet. Notice especially the movement of attention in your head. Remember your brain is the seat of the mind and tension and tightness are arising right there. Release and relax in one gentle motion. Just a touch of the 6Rs is enough. Back away quickly from any movement of mind. It can even be the slightest sensation that draws your attention. Relax right then.

At this stage, mind will be serene and bright. There is a brightness of mind with clear, energetic mindfulness. You are progressing well. You easily see anything arising. You relax into any distractions and 6R automatically. Your mind simply has no thoughts, and your attention never wanders.

The subtlest links of dependent origination will start to appear in your awareness. First, there are the consciousnesses arising from the deep inner mind. Then even deeper are the formations which are the cause of those consciousnesses. You are not this phenomenon arising. Don't identify with it. It is craving. Now, just peace of mind without these vibrations and movements of mind is what you are now finding more desirable. There is less suffering in this quiet, tranquil mind. Less is better.

What are formations? They are defined as bodily, verbal and mental formations. They are very small movements. They are the potentials of actions to arise and not the full-fledged results. These are the little "seeds" out of which consciousness arises. These, in turn, lead to mentality-materiality, and then to the arising of the sense bases. Then, with contact, they explode into conscious awareness.

We won't mention here how they appear because we want you to tell the teacher what you think you are seeing. The teacher will decide if you are right. We don't want to put any expectation here. It is important for you to see deeply on your own without preconceptions. If there is no teacher available, it still doesn't matter as to whatever arises; the instruction is to always 6R and go back to your meditation object. You still must let go of everything.

When you see what you think are the formations or some deeper links, 6R them as you would any other phenomena. By 6Ring any link that arises, this will uncover the next link deeper in the chain. We are removing tension and tightness from the craving in the links as they arise — and when we do, this reveals the next deeper part. How do you 6R ignorance? You don't. It is an understanding of the four noble truths.

In Sutta MN 128 "Imperfections," the Buddha states that the meditator may have the brightness and light fall away. What would be the reason for the loss of brightness? But, of course, it would be those pesky hindrances arising! They are dark clouds gathering over this bright clear mind. Sometimes mind is so clear that it can be described as "luminous."

Many times, sitting in this state restlessness might come up since there is not much to observe. You may want something to watch and might want to start to control things. Boredom can arise, along with a corresponding lessening of mindfulness. Because of this, the light recedes. Balancing the factors of energy — tranquility, mindfulness, and the other awakening factors — once again will bring that radiant mind back.

Continue to use a clear mind as your object of meditation. If your mindfulness is strong, there will mostly be the quiet. Now and then some slight activity will arise. Mind will start to vibrate, and there will be a pulling away from the quiet mind — this balanced still-point where your awareness resides. 6R right then and come back to the quiet. Your goal is a completely unmoving mind. Just know and understand what is happening and relax. Know you are right here in the Quiet Present. Understand this at every moment-lightly.

Your object of meditation continues to be that quiet mind itself. Be on the lookout for any activity that arises. If you feel you are losing the quiet, you can bring up that feeling of stillness and notice this. When your mind quiets down again, then you can let go of that feeling and go back to just observing and relaxing into mind's subtle movements.

The Neutral Zone

Gradually, even the smallest bits of mental activity will subside. It will be as if there is nothing to 6R at all. You may get restless and want to get up. It is like you feel there is nothing left to do. Do not do that. 6R that restlessness and keep sitting! Now is the time for patience and persistence. Very little happens. You have to be okay with that. Mind will settle down more and more if you just continue. You might not even realize progress is being made, but it is.

If restlessness or any hindrance starts to get the upper hand just observe with the intention, "I don't care what happens next; my job is just to observe what is there."

You will see the subtlest aspects of mind. In it are the seeds, or potentials, that ultimately lead to birth, old age, and death.

The teacher will ask questions to find out what you are seeing. You will be advised to be very watchful as to how the movements arise and how they appear. And you should not take them personally! They are not "your" movements arising; they just are phenomena coming from mind. We don't know why and we don't care; our only job is to allow and relax into them as they fade away.

It is important for mindfulness and tranquility to continue to develop so that these very slight phenomena can be seen and understood. Eventually, you will see all of the links except Ignorance (which is just something that you will come to understand), and, as well, you will see all the Four Noble Truths.

You are working your way backward, letting go of each link by going deeper and deeper. You will see the link mentality-materiality, and continue backward to consciousness, and then the formations. You will be advised to 6R these objects when they appear, uncovering the next link. There is the separate and big *craving* link itself, after *feeling* and before *clinging,* in the twelve links, but there is also a small amount of craving in each individual link, keeping the wheel of Samsarā turning. You will be able to see all of that. You will see the entire process of mind.

As you 6R deeper and deeper, you will be advised to keep backing away from each object that arises. Every time there is a sound, the chain of dependent origination fires off, and you will want to 6R all of that. Look at the links arising closer and closer to see how each tiny part of it arises. There is craving there to let go.

You need to let everything that arises come by itself; don't look for it. In this way, you can see how there might be a craving to go look for more experience.

Your mind constantly wants to go forward and, like Pac-Man, engage in more and more senses to see what is there — to live more, to experience more. This happens because whatever is experienced passes away. So, mind is constantly looking for more to replace the phenomena that have just passed. See if you can see this jumping from object to object by taking a mental standpoint of a full-stop. Just mentally standing still and letting all experience pass through your imperturbable state of mind which doesn't react, not even to the slightest puff of vibration.

We are exiting this roundabout existence (saṃsāra). We do this by letting go, by seeing clearly each link as it arises, and by seeing it as impersonal, impermanent, and unsatisfactory.

MN: 111 section 18. Cont. "So indeed, these states, not having been, come into being; having been, they vanish. Regarding those states, he abided unattracted, unrepelled, independent, detached, free, dissociated, with a mind rid of barriers. He understood: 'There is an escape beyond,' and with the cultivation of that attainment, he confirmed that there is."

Disenchantment

While in this quiet and clear state of mind, there comes first the knowledge of Disenchantment. Up to now, you have continued to observe phenomena arising and passing away with some interest. You notice you are getting deeper, so you keep going. There is less and less to 6R as you go along. Mind becomes quieter and quieter.

As you continue, you notice this constant arising and passing away of objects. You notice the silent space between the objects that arise and pass away. You think to yourself, "What if I could get rid of these objects coming and going? Then there would be just the peace." You think that then there would be only silence and not all these annoying objects and vibrations. You see the lack of ease as suffering.

This trying to control has an aspect of longing in it. Wanting to have something happen is the very thing that will stop it. The teacher will remind the student that their job is simply to observe.

You realize that now you are beginning to develop a whole new perspective on the world. You had never thought that the lack of mental activity would be good, but now you do! You see that any mental activity and movement is unsatisfactory; silence is better. Now you see any vibration, and even any consciousness, as unsatisfactory. You even try to stop things from arising and you can't! You were never in control at all; it just keeps coming!

Your mind starts to go toward silence, but there is a problem. The mental stream doesn't stop and just keeps on rolling. A subtle sort of observation arises: "I am really tired of these sensations disturbing my peace of mind." Dissatisfaction arises along with the realization that it would be best to see all these arising phenomena just stop, "let me, please have some peace." You are starting to become disenchanted.

You look for a reason why these constant sensations and mental objects arise, but there seems to be none. If you could find the reason, then you might be able to understand why it comes, or a way to turn it off. You want to analyze and solve the problem, but you don't see a solution.

Finally, you just give up looking. Interest in watching this constant stream starts to wane. You realize there really is no end to it. This is an arising state of knowledge about your mind and the life process: It will never end. There is no peace here.

> *"There was total disinterest in the impermanence of "I" and insight into the silliness of identifying a non-existent permanent "I" with every feeling, thought and action. Deeper experiential realization that feelings and thoughts were not under my control; that thoughts or mind objects, in general, were like what odors were to the nose, or sounds were to the ears. They came and went without me being involved. I continued to 6R nonetheless. S.D. California*

You are energetic, continually watching every little vibration, thought form, etc., and you can be very determined to relax and let go of everything that arises. By doing that, you think you will get to the end of the process — but it doesn't work.

You now understand all that arises to be a disturbance. It upsets the quiet state of mind that you are starting to enjoy — enjoy not in a craving sort of way but with appreciation. You are starting to relish the quiet. You understand that balance is better than chasing more objects. This realization will lead to contentment; contentment will arise without the cascade of vibrations and movements constantly assaulting you.

You may have some desire for Nibbāna to arise and might think you are close. Then you might put too much energy in and start to lean into the future, hoping for the attainment to arise. You need to 6R this desire. This is the arising of more craving. This is longing.

You may think that you need to have the desire to reach the goal. No, you have already pointed your mind there. Let the meditation do the rest. You make a determination about getting somewhere, and then you just go. You don't think about the destination the whole time you are on the way there. You just continue, trusting that it will happen as planned because you are on the right path. This is determination.

Is the desire for Nibbāna something that we should not have? In these final sessions of sitting before attaining awakening, we need to let go of even the desire for Nibbāna. When we first start, however, we won't even begin the meditation without some intentional desire to get us on the path. So, it is a positive desire, a wholesome desire. Because, after all, it is a desire for no desire. It is not like a desire for chocolate ice cream or a new car. It is a desire to stop and be still and know peace. This kind of wholesome desire is called *Chanda* in Pāli.

As was stated above, you don't know how to stop this stuff from coming and coming. You want it to stop. There is nothing but vibration at all different levels. Now you see peace as a more desirable goal. Now you wish to be void of these sensations.

Finally, there comes the point where you just stop caring about all these arising phenomena. You can't command this stream to stop. You start to give up and see that by paying heed to the phenomena, you are feeding them. They will never stop if you are interested in what is there. You realize that all this movement and vibration is disturbing your collectedness and peace.

Mind now becomes disinterested in what arises, and there is a deeper feeling of disenchantment. There are endless arisings. This is suffering. This is dukkha, which is Pāli for suffering or dis-ease. The Buddha said the First Noble Truth of existence is suffering. Now you see it. You see how you pay attention to and like and dislike everything that arises, thereby keeping it going through craving — the Second Noble Truth. Now you see the goal — the Cessation of Craving is the cessation of suffering, the third noble truth.

Dispassion

This leads to an even deeper letting go: dispassion arises. Disenchantment made you more and more aware of how your interest in these things just leads to more suffering; now you just don't care anymore. It doesn't matter what comes or goes. Your mind draws back; it doesn't look outward anymore. Everything that arises is okay; it doesn't matter. It no longer pulls your attention. You know you can't stop it. You don't even care about Nibbāna anymore.

This is a state where there are no more hindrances. Your mind has just stopped throwing up obstacles. It has no more interest in any arising experience now. You no longer try to control anything. You are now close to the unconditioned! Why? Because you don't care.

Through disenchantment with all conditioned existence, a wholly balanced mind arises. It neither likes nor dislikes. There are only consciousnesses and mental objects arising and passing away. There is no interest in any of it. It is just there. There is now the tendency toward deep peace of mind. Your mind now has barely any movement at all. You are very aware and very energetic, but again it's like nothing is happening, and the thought comes up where you wonder if you should do anything. The answer is definitely no. Just observe. See that very question arising in your mind as impersonal and 6R it.

It is just a matter of time, watching and observing carefully for any movement like flickers, lights or just vibrations. The 6Rs are on automatic, and you aren't putting in much effort — it just rolls off in front of you. You will observe this lack of hindrances, but it won't make you excited — it is just part of what is happening. It is nonetheless amazing! To have no unwholesome states at all; to be free of craving completely. This realization has all come through your own deep insights into watching yourself coming into and out of existence.

When dispassion arises, you will be very close. You think there is nothing left to do because there is nothing to 6R, so you want to get up and do something else. There are no more barriers to the meditation. Why continue? You think everything has been completed.

But, just continue and be patient with this sublimely quiet mind. Continue to observe without even caring about what comes up anymore. You have realized now there is nothing that "you" can do about it. "Patience leads to Nibbāna."

This path is not just one step after another until you reach the goal. You will have doubts; you will get out of balance with your observational power. Then you will figure it out. Two steps forward and one step back.

If you are not progressing further and you seem to hit a wall, you should ask yourself, your intuition, "What is stopping my meditation from going deeper?" The answer may come the next hour or the next day. Sometimes there are blockages that are hidden and simply not discoverable by the teacher if you are working with one, or by you.

Hopefully, an answer will come back. You may be applying too much energy. You may need to back away further from everything. Or you may not be observant enough in seeing how the links arise, how you take things personally and identify with them. You may be leaning into the process too much.

Bhante Vimalaramsi speaks about one student who asked himself this question. He just posed it to himself. Later, the answer came back that he was "waiting." Waiting for what? "Waiting for Nibbāna." The waiting was the problem. There was craving there, and that had to be released.

Whatever is stopping you will eventually yield as your knowledge deepens. Sometimes this blockage can go on for a long time. Gradually, even if it takes years of retreats, you mature your technique and knowledge of how to do the practice.

Some people will understand easily, follow the instructions, and apply them. In only a matter of days or weeks, they break through to awakening. They fall into the stream of the Noble Ones. Patience, and following the instructions precisely, does lead to Nibbāna!

"At a certain point, mind was very still, and there was drifting into a deep lucid sleep - mind was fully aware and alert, however. Then, towards the end, I blanked out completely, like I lost consciousness, and there was no feeling or perception. I only seemed to be aware that I blanked out after coming out from it. But the blanking out was only for a little time before I came back to this lucid deep sleep state.

Emerging from this meditation, mind was totally still, alert, and automatically radiating equanimity. Everything I did after the meditation had a very calm, smooth, and mindful quality. People noticed I took time with my words and responses to them and seemed very relaxed. Indeed, I felt very relaxed; mind was totally balanced. Very strong equanimity throughout the day." S.D. California

Let's go to the Majjhima Nikāya to see even more clearly how the Buddha described this process in sutta 148, "The Six Sets of Six." In the first 80 percent of the text, the Buddha describes the impersonality of each sense base as it arises and passes away. Nothing is you, consciousness is not you, your body is not you, and so on. Toward the end, he tells the students that as they observe, they will come to understand certain insights as well as why they arise.

Liberation (from Sutta MN 148)

MN:148 Section 40: "Seeing thus, monks, a well-taught disciple becomes disenchanted with the eye, disenchanted with forms, disenchanted with eye-consciousness, disenchanted with eye-contact, disenchanted with eye-feeling, disenchanted with eye-craving."

It says that now the student starts to pull away, starts to understand there is nothing in this arising and passing show in which to delight. What does the student really see here? The sutta tells us:

MN148: Section 39: "Students, dependent on mind and mind-objects, mind-consciousness arises; the meeting of the three is mind-contact; with mind-contact as condition there arises a mind feeling felt as pleasant or painful or neither-pleasant-nor-painful.

When one is touched by a pleasant mind-feeling, if one does not delight in it, welcome it, and remain holding to it, then the underlying tendency to lust does not lie within one.

When one is touched by a painful mind-feeling, if one does not sorrow, grieve, and lament, does not weep beating one's breast and become distraught, then the underlying tendency to aversion does not lie within one.

When one is touched by a neither-pleasant-nor-painful mind-feeling, if one understands it as it is — the origination, the disappearance, the gratification, the danger, and the escape in regard to that mind-feeling — then the underlying tendency to ignorance does not lie within one."

As you watch mind and mind objects coming and going, you are interested in this process; you are delighting in this observation — in seeing how it all works. The feeling of delight is so subtle you may not understand it as such, but you do like watching it and trying to figure out why the process arises and what this all means.

At times mind is kind of fun to watch. Through this "gratification" (which is defined as "source of pleasure"), you watch and try to get to the goal but you can't. There is the tendency to lust after these arising and disappearing objects. Or you push them away as interfering with your calm — or you have indifference and don't care about them. It is the craving mind that takes this indifference *personally*. It is *your* indifference. It is not a clear, pure mind.

In other words, you see the arising and passing of many objects, and you are attracted. Then only if you see that these objects are sources of pleasure or aversion will you see the *danger* to your mind by chasing and lusting after them, as this leads to suffering, old-age, and death!

When disenchantment arises, the Buddha goes on to say:

MN:148 sections 35-39. "Monks, that one shall here and now make an end of suffering by abandoning the underlying tendency to lust for pleasant mind-feeling, by abolishing the underlying tendency to aversion for painful mind-feeling, by extirpating {uprooting} the underlying tendency to ignorance in regard to neither-pleasant-nor-painful mind-feeling, by abandoning ignorance and arousing true knowledge — this is possible."

By giving up your tendency toward delighting in this or that, and your tendency to lust after these delights, by seeing the danger in it and so on, you come to the end of desire.

You no longer want to keep chasing these feelings as they only lead to suffering. And it's not because you are forcing restraint on yourself, it is because you are no longer delighted by this "passing show." You no longer care.

Thus, dispassion to all phenomena arises through the knowledge of craving (the Four Noble Truths) and how craving leads to suffering. Freedom from the wheel of saṃsāra is experienced. All that had to be done is done. The door to Nibbāna is opening.

Entering the Stream

Now, we arrive at the attainments and how Nibbāna is experienced. First, I will describe the four levels of "noble attainments" to be experienced. You must go through all four to be fully awakened and free of craving. Craving drops away in stages.

In total, there are four "stages of sainthood:" Sotāpanna, Sakadāgāmī, Anāgāmī, and Arahant. Each of the four stages has two components. The Path Knowledge (magga) and the Fruition Knowledge (phala).

Path Knowledge is the first glimpse of Nibbāna but still may be lost if precepts are not followed. Once the Fruit Knowledge is gained the attainment is locked in and cannot be lost.

There are eight attainments in all to final awakening, two for each of the major stages of sainthood (path and fruit). At the last one the last fetter of all ten "fetters of craving" is destroyed.

Three are eliminated at Sotāpanna, two more are loosened at Sakadāgāmī, and finally, all of the *first* five fetters are let go at Anāgāmi. The balance of the ten is eliminated at Arahant.

What are the fetters? With awakening, the hindrances are abandoned once and for all. But there remain subtler, innate unwholesome tendencies in all of us that are born from craving. The word "fetter" is defined as something that restrains us. These are the final chains that bind us to this endless round of existences. The fetters are the last potentials of unwholesome states. I will list them as we go through the noble paths and note where they are eliminated.

Chapter Fifteen:
1st Stage of Awakening — Sotāpanna

MN:111 section 19. "Again, monks, by completely surmounting the base of neither-perception-nor-non-perception, Sāriputta entered upon and abided in the cessation of perception and feeling.

Attaining Nibbāna – Path Knowledge (Magga)

Finally, after staying with this quiet, energetic, imperturbable mind of the base of neither-perception-nor-non-perception, and 6Ring every tiny movement until mind is barely moving at all, you let go of the last *condition*, the last link of ignorance, and all activity ceases. Everything stops and an *unconditioned* state arises.

There is the cessation of perception, feeling, and consciousness, for a few moments or minutes. You don't know you're in that state until after you come out. Some will say they experienced a "blank spot" or a "gap" in consciousness. This is nothing like any of your previous jhāna experiences. It isn't a gap with a sense of time because there is nothing missing — time doesn't exist when nothing is happening — there is just the stopping of the stream of consciousness, a halting. You only know it after you come out of it. The world stops, you are no longer in saṃsāra — and it will last as long as it's going to last.

Does life still exist? Vitality and your life continuum still go on. Your autonomic functions like your heart beating and blood pumping continue. But your mental process has stopped completely.

"When I finished radiating Equanimity to each of the points something extremely new happened: A feeling I had felt in a meditation

a couple a days ago but it was now much clearer and more defined: <u>*In a second it was as if a membrane around me totally broke and*</u> <u>*released me. One second.*</u> *From there, a huge space opened up before me, the feeling that there was so much room, there were no barriers. At the same moment my face begins to fade ... As if something was literally erasing it... (and left me without skin or muscles). There was happiness, but without excitement. Tranquility and a very, very refined attention."* Barcelona, Spain

Before, there just existed slight movements of mind. But now with this temporary cessation of all mental activity there arises right after that a powerful clarity of mind. You have just had the deepest "rest" of your life. When you come back you are now seeing the subtlest movements, deeper than you have ever experienced. Mind appears like a totally erased blackboard. Nothing is on it. Then, when mind turns back on, the first mental process is clearly seen against this inky black background.

Coming out of cessation, mind is radiant and observant. You have arrived at full stop. The effect of the cessation is so powerful that whereas before the pond of your mind had tiny little ripples on it, now it is so still and placid that you can see anything there — you can see to any depth what is below. There is no craving at all. There is no "dust" to obscure vision. Mind is so pure that you see the smallest detail of anything that starts to arise in crystal clarity. What you are about to see is the first arising of consciousness — the first moment of mental activity.

As your mental processes begin again from this still point, the next thing that happens is that you see the links of dependent origination arise and pass away very quickly. These are sometimes in the form of vibrations or little lights, flashes, or electrical currents. You will see this in your mind and sometimes even see it in the air in front of you. You won't know what it is, very likely, and will not expect it. This is the first conditioned mental process in which your mind starts to vibrate again and come back "online."

When this happens, the eye of wisdom (mind without craving) sees the total impersonality of the process. There is no self there. Your deep observation understands that there is *nobody home*, that what "you" are is just a process of moments arising and passing away. As a result of this profound insight, the supra-mundane unconditioned Nibbāna arises.

This experience will be followed by a momentary sense of relief like a burden was lifted off. You have just experienced Nibbāna! You have become a Sotāpanna.

"In meditation things began to slow down. The vibrations slowed to a ripple that ended in bright light. I went deeper and things seemed slower, there seemed to be something breaking up in the light. I went even deeper until the distractions abruptly stopped, like the plug had been pulled out. Mind activity abruptly stopped, what was left was like a blackout, the centre seemed darker than the edges. For a moment it felt like something was missing. I didn't feel joy, more like a calm relief." C.B. Sri Lanka

Nibbāna will not come when you want it — it will come when you are ready — when the seven factors of awakening all line up in perfect balance, like passing through the keyhole of the door. You didn't think it could be possible, yet it happened.

You see that, in this seemingly permanent and eternal psychophysical process, when mind stops, there really is nothing between each thought moment that persists. That knowledge leads you to understand that an impersonal underlies everything. There is nothing that is continuous between each moment, nothing that survives. Not even God. Nothing. Everything is absolutely void of self or soul.

MN:111 section 19 cont. "And his taints were destroyed by his seeing with wisdom."

The word here is *wisdom*. So, what is wisdom? After the cessation of perception, feeling, and consciousness — and it's going to last as long as it will last — when feeling, perception and consciousness start up again, you have the opportunity of seeing exactly, clearly, with very sharp mindfulness, every one of the links of dependent origination. You will see how when this doesn't arise, that doesn't arise; that each link is dependent on the previous link. You will see that everything has a cause for arising. You have uncovered the last link of ignorance.

You will also see that if it arises, it will come to an end. You will see impermanence clearly. All that arises will pass away whether it be pleasure or pain.

This is wisdom. It is the knowledge that you gain by directly seeing the links of dependent origination arise and pass away and by seeing that there is no enduring self. This wisdom is not some sort of conceptual philosophy, some religious tenet or dogma — it is the result of seeing directly. When you see the word "wisdom" in the suttas, you should understand that this always means seeing the links of dependent origination directly and seeing everything that arises as impersonal. It isn't learning a philosophy; it is directly observing reality.

With the next mental process that arises, you will see the whole arising and passing away of all of the links of dependent origination for the duration of one instant. Then there is the final letting go of ignorance and seeing the Four Noble Truths; that is when Nibbāna occurs.

It is just a momentary event and just one group of links firing. The links are seen with *Wisdom's Eye*. This takes place at a deeper level than normal awareness.

People will say they don't know what they saw, but they will *know.* Their mind, to a greater or lesser degree, will be having insights arise into how there is a cause that creates a result. This constant arising and passing away of conditioned existence is the content of who we are — and that's all there is. They will now understand at an intuitive level how dependent origination works.

Each link is conditioned by the previous link. Each process is conditioned by the passing away of another process — like a candle flame that lights another candle. One candle burns down, but the next candle lights up, being ignited by the previous candle.

Bit by bit "you" arise and pass away. You are changing little by little over time. Like a great city that arises from an empty piece of land ,each building arises one at a time. Each shovel of dirt carried off and dumped one at a time. With the constant arising and passing away of causes, this great city is built. The next shovelful of dirt taken away changes it once again. No one person has built it — just many shovels and people shoveling. It's a process with no real beginning and no real end.

We give cities names, but these are just concepts to label these groups of buildings. The perception aggregate of the five aggregates is partially memory and part labeling. *Perception* is what puts a name on this group of buildings. It labels it either New York or San Francisco depending on what, for example, visual forms arise.

In our own case, we are given a name, like John, and then we personally identify with that name as if some underlying entity were controlling everything. But it isn't. It is just a concept.

The city itself is not one solid thing. It is the result of all these causes that make it what it is — but in this instant only. In the next moment, it has changed to something else.

In the same way, "you" are a completely impersonal process — there is no *one* or soul behind it. It is automatically happening and will continue forever into the future until you become fully awake and exit the wheel of saṃsāra. This is so profound that after these links pass away, Nibbāna arises just for an instant. In the suttas it says, **"..and his *taints* were destroyed with wisdom,"** meaning that

Nibbāna arises right after you see the links of dependent origination, and it destroys a certain measured amount of craving. It destroys the first three, what are called, fetters.

Step-by-Step Attainment of Nibbāna

- The cessation of feeling, perception, and consciousness occurs. This means that everything we consider a person stops. There is a blank state, a blackout or voidness. All mental activity stops. On an EEG one would guess the indicator flatlines for just a moment.

- Following the cessation, because of the incredible clarity created by the experience of cessation, the first mental activity — a set of twelve links — arises and passes away. They might be seen like bubbles or little flashing lights.

- Wisdom's Eye observes utter and total *impersonality* in this first mental process as the links arise and pass away. With no craving to cloud mind, the links are seen as just an impersonal process with no inherent self. Just a group of neurons firing! That is all "you" are!

- After the last link of ignorance passes away, Nibbāna arises.

- There is a feeling of *Relief* for a moment — a unique feeling in the mind that there has been a great burden thrown off.

- Joy starts to arise — all-pervading joy that can last for up to several days. It may continue longer, but sometimes you just get used to the state and don't notice it anymore. Note that the *Relief* and the *Joy* that follows are different feelings. You should notice this difference.

"There was definitely joy, but I think what followed was the mind jumping for a brief moment, "Oh wow, what just happened!" because it was not like the nothingness between the flickering of consciousness, and yet pervading joy persisted after the blanking out

and continued even after the meditation. This kind of joy I couldn't compare to drunkenness although I can see how people might do so because if I caught myself in the mirror, my eyes were just so relaxed, and I had a wide smile on my face. It's of a different quality. I think Bhante once called it relief, and I could definitely apply that to it.

Mind was totally equanimous and relaxed and balanced and only focused on what the body was doing, no matter how mundane. For example, when I went to put pizza in the oven, there were no reflections or thoughts, or anything in the mind. My focus was on unboxing the pizza, slowly, almost like an automaton, without any involvement yet I was totally present and aware of each action happening. S. D. California

The first time Nibbāna occurs, many people will not recognize or see the twelve links, but they will have the experience of Nibbāna regardless. At the next level called *Fruition*, it is likely they will witness more clearly the links arising and passing away; fruition knowledge is much deeper. It happens in this way, for many people, when they experience the first path. The Sotāpanna Path Knowledge can have the cessation with the relief, but the links themselves just are not clear. They may report more often a blackout where they just "disappeared" and then came back.

The Fruition will be attained later after they have practiced some more. This will cement in the attainment in a deeper way.

Again, when wisdom arises, the first three of the ten fetters are eliminated in the First Path attainment. All of the fetters are fully abandoned after the attainment of full awakening, which is Arahantship.

What is Nibbāna? Nibbāna is described in the Pāli texts as a *dhātu* or "element" (earth, air, fire, water, space and consciousness are elements as taught by the Buddha). The Nibbāna *dhātu* is also an element, and its other qualities are described by Bhikkhu Bodhi here:

"The Buddha also refers to Nibbāna as a 'āyatana.' This means realm, plane, or sphere. It is a sphere where there is nothing at all that corresponds to our mundane experience, and therefore it has to be described by way of negations as the negation of all the limited and determinate qualities of conditioned things.

The Buddha also refers to Nibbāna as a 'dhātu,' an element, the 'deathless element.' He compares the element of Nibbāna to an ocean. He says that just as the great ocean remains at the same level no matter how much water pours into it from the rivers, without increase or decrease, so the Nibbāna element remains the same, no matter whether many or few people attain Nibbāna.

He also speaks of Nibbāna as something that can be experienced by the body, an experience that is so vivid, so powerful, that it can be described as 'touching the deathless element with one's own body.'

The Buddha also refers to Nibbāna as a 'state' (pada) as 'amatapada' — the deathless state — or accutapada, the imperishable state.

Another word used by the Buddha to refer to Nibbāna is 'Sacca,' which means 'truth,' an existing reality. This refers to Nibbāna as the truth, a reality that the Noble ones have known through direct experience.

So, all these terms, considered as a whole, clearly establish that Nibbāna is an actual reality and not the mere destruction of defilements or the cessation of existence. Nibbāna is unconditioned, without any origination and is timeless."[xiv]

When the Nibbāna element touches craving, it is like the water of the Great Ocean putting the fire out. Pssss.... No more fire. Ni means "no," and bāna means "fire." No fire. Nibbāna.

Venerable Buddhadasa Bhikkhu in an article entitled, Nibbāna for Everyone: A Truth Message from Suan Mokkh (adapted and translated by Santikaro Bhikkhu) also defines Nibbāna as an element:

"It is the coolness when the defilements are ended...Nibbāna was a whole other matter than death. Instead, it's a kind of life that knows no death. Nibbāna is the thing which sustains life, thus preventing death. It itself can never die, although the body must die eventually."

The cessation and the experience of Nibbāna are two different things. Some say when mind stops that is Nibbāna. No, it is what happens afterword which is seeing the links arise that causes the profound insight into existence to arise. That is Nibbāna.

We can't describe the experiences of Nibbāna that happens in each path of sainthood with conditioned words, as it is beyond our conceptual mind to perceive. But it is what comes *after* the experience that gives you a clue as to what has just happened.

As described before some explain feeling a moment of relief after it happens. Some experience a deep understanding of dependent origination. Some say they just went away into a "black hole" or disappeared.

Then, slowly, a mild to strong euphoria arises. I am careful not to use the word "joy" here, it is beyond that. Some describe it like steam that ascends slowly in mind or perhaps a "minty" feeling. This is what we call *all-pervading joy*; it seeps out from every pore of your body. You may not notice it at first, but soon you feel very uplifted and elevated. It is a feeling of happiness but grounded in very strong equanimity.

You realize, in a flash, that there is no controller. There is no ego. There is no self — everything is impersonal.

It is said, "No self, no problem!" What a relief! There is nothing to worry about or control. It is all impersonal — arising and passing away on its own. All of these mental states are arising from causes. They are just conditioned by previous actions. In fact, the meaning of *kamma* (Pāli) or *karma* (Sanskrit) is action. There is the action and then the result from that action (*vipāka*).

There is no self that you need to psychoanalyze to get to the *real problem* of this depression or neurosis! Once the concept of self is gone there is nobody left to be depressed, or more clearly, nobody left to take a painful feeling personally. It is only a feeling and it isn't your feeling.

You may notice that everything looks a little different now. Your senses appear to be heightened more than normal meditation might make them. Colors are brighter, or you just find yourself looking at the trees with awe and wonder. You notice the mind is sublimely quiet.

You will be asked if you notice a change in your personality. Do you feel different? Do you have a change in perspective? For some, it is a dramatic change, and for others, it is subtler.

"In terms of perception, yes, I can see a noticeable shift - everything that's happening around me no longer has my emotional involvement, good, bad or indifferent. There's a visible and experiential impersonal nature to the events around me, and my mind is no longer reacting to things.

I'm taking my time with things, not in a rush - there's nowhere to go, what's the hurry - and there's a pleasantness pervading my actions, calm, collected and happy!" S. D. California

You will say your mind feels very relieved and happy. You talk about how you understand now how everything arises due to causes and conditions. You are starting to understand deeply what the links are and how they are dependent on each other. Instead of understanding them intellectually you now understand them directly.

You may use the simile of the cloth as the Buddha did: how everything — with its causes and conditions — weaves together to make a cloth. It is all impersonal. *Sutta* means "thread" in Pāli; all the suttas weaved together to make the cloth. The cloth represents your wise understanding of the whole process of the Buddha's teaching.

"Prior to it (the experience) I felt gradual changes after each sitting like anger reducing and catching some thoughts half way. After the blackout, anger, worries, stress etc. seem to be massively reduced - peace of mind. Occasionally negative things would arise, and I could feel a slight tension that I would relax but didn't require too much manual intervention.

Also, unlike earlier where I was catching them half way through I was aware of them much earlier. My senses seem more acute, smells are stronger, colours seem brighter and I'm seeing details I didn't before." C.B. Sri Lanka

You may or may not remember seeing very much of this, but you will know it — this is Wisdom's Eye. The profound knowledge from directly seeing. The deep mind sees what happened, and it has understood what it means. This is Wisdom — seeing the links of dependent origination. This is the Path knowledge. You are now on the path to the full experience of the first stage of awakening.

Decisions arise in your mind, and you commit an action that has a result, like a painful or pleasant feeling arising in the future. Breaking precepts results in painful consequences. Following precepts result in wholesome, pleasant results. What results do you want? Now you know what is wholesome and what leads to wholesome.

Most people will experience the first path knowledge in a sitting meditation, but some have reported that it happened after washing dishes or even turning over and going back to sleep. Nibbāna happens when your knowledge is mature, and you are ready.

At the meditation center in Missouri, we see people get the path attainment every now and then, and one of the principal ways you can tell is that their face changes. It is like all the tension from a lifetime just disappears. It looks as though the face drops — the wrinkled forehead flattens out. You can just see the equanimity bubbling; there is a glowing and a radiance that is there; their speech is more controlled and less emotional.

Many times, Bhante, after he comes from the interviews, will point out a meditator to me and say, "Look at their face." When I look, if I look close enough, I see an emotionless but peaceful, angelic expression or just a big smile with a glowing radiance that wasn't there before.

After a few days, the most dramatic of these effects disappears as the hindrances make their way back — just not as strong as before.

"Started off radiating equanimity, which was strong right after walking with radiating equanimity. Immediately went into Nei-ther-Perception-nor-Non-Perception. No desire, no craving for anything, just allowing mind to relax deeper and deeper and deeper while staying on Quiet Mind. A [cessation] blank occurred and immediately after emergence, stayed in 8th jhāna for a while, then came out and continued to 6R.

The joy and equanimity that followed was refreshing. The view of the world around has changed drastically. There is non-attachment and non-aversion, as I'm just staying with quiet mind, smiling without effort and radiating compassion to others. I've noticed I'm unable to break the precepts, in that I'm automatically following them without a second thought and without effort. Sense of "me" has just vanished. The world is seriously different in the way it is experienced since I began this retreat.

Sensual pleasures are nothing compared to the meditation and being unhappy seems like an impossibility. There is tremendous silence in the mind and interactions with others are joyful and happy with lots of laughing and delightful words, all the while radiating loving-kindness to them. Attachment or aversion make no sense at all when there's no one being attached or feeling aversion and no thoughts in the mind. Sense of ownership too has faded.

There's nothing to own or keep. What comes, comes and what goes, goes. If it comes, okay. If it goes, okay too.

I'm in automatic happiness mode - everything that happens around me can be good or bad or nothing at all - and I can just smile, laugh and be happy for no reason. There's no sense of tiredness or lethargy - who is being tired? Moreover, coming out of the meditation seems to generate a lot of energy for the day - it's better than any energy drink or coffee.

Craving has become minuscule - it just doesn't register as something the mind can do anymore." S. D. California

Sotāpanna Fruition (Phala)

The First Path knowledge, which is experienced one time, is followed by the First Fruition Knowledge. The Path knowledge gets you through the door; the Fruition Knowledge closes the door and locks in your understanding. This all happens when you have another cessation moment arise in your meditation, and you experience Nibbāna again.

After you experience the Sotāpanna Path attainment as outlined above, then if you sit and continue to meditate exactly as you did before, you will experience that process of a blank spot and flashes again, with another feeling of relief. This is the Sotāpanna Fruition. This is the first stage of four stages of sainthood.

You have entered the temple now, but there are three more levels of attainment following Sotāpanna which we will get into following this chapter.

However, you might be too restless to sit right after your path attainment. This is due to the strong all-pervading joy you will be experiencing. Over the next few days, as your energy wanes, you will be encouraged to go back to your chair or cushion and gain the *fruition* of Sotāpanna. You may be told that your mind is very strong now. Do not waste any time. Use this time to make even more progress.

You are understandably happy about your Path experience. But now that your mind is bright and very clear, it is helpful to continue to the Fruit of the first stage of awakening. Your mind is open and ready, so just continue with your practice.

Gaining the Fruit is what changes the personality in a major way. Gaining the First Path is a preliminary step to gaining the full attainment and fruition of Sotāpanna.

The meditator with only the Path experience can actually slide back due to bad behavior in breaking precepts. You can lose your attainment. This is why it is called the Path knowledge. You have become a *cula Sotāpanna* (little stream enterer); you are still on the Path — but you are not done yet. You must keep the precepts fully, meditate, and attain cessation once again.

Once the Fruition is attained, the path has been fully traveled, and you are now a *Noble* one who will never break the precepts. You have reached the first level of Sainthood. Bhante Vimalaraṁsi likes to say you have given up "an ocean of suffering!"

A Sotāpanna purifies and eliminates from his mind the first three fetters of being (there are ten in all):

1. ***Sakkāya-diṭṭhi:*** *personality belief. You now know, without any doubt, that there is no permanent self or soul.*

2. ***Vicikicchā:*** *skeptical doubt about the Dhamma. You will have no doubt about the path. You will know how you achieved what you did and how to continue the practice. You have total confidence in the Buddha's method. You have full confidence in the Buddha, Dhamma, and Sangha.*

3. ***Sīlabbataparāmāsa:*** *clinging to rites and rituals, thinking that they will, by themselves, lead to awakening. You will understand that bowing, chanting, or worshiping the Buddha will not get you to the experience of Nibbāna, no matter how much you do this. You must do the work of meditation and*

study to attain Nibbāna.

With the second step of Fruition being attained, you will not be able to break precepts anymore. You might try to do it, just as a test, but you won't be able to go through with it. With only the Path knowledge you could potentially break them, and this is the danger of not attaining the Fruit.

With only the first path knowledge it is still possible that if you did continue to break precepts and behave badly, you could "lose" your attainment. You would have to go through the process, having the experience of seeing dependent origination, again. Sutta MN 105 Sunakkhatta sutta addresses this possibility with the simile of the wound and healing. If one does not take care of the wound, it is liable to become infected, however, with proper care the wound will heal completely without any possibility of becoming infected. In the same way with the proper taking care of Path Knowledge, your attainment will not be lost.

With the Fruition, your attainment is locked in. There is no going back to the state of the worldling (*puthujjana*).

As a Sotāpanna you are destined to have no more than seven lifetimes before you get off the wheel, become a full Arahant with all ten fetters destroyed, and attain final *parinibbāna*. Also, when you are reborn, at worst you will not fall below the human realm. You are also assured that your next life will be pleasant, where you can continue to do your work to get off the wheel.

There are thirty-one planes of existences. You will not fall into the painful, hellish realms now. You won't come back as an animal or ghost. You may return to the human realm, or to one of the six Deva or Celestial Heaven realms where there is only enjoyment and pleasures. If you attained jhāna (and you certainly did practicing TWIM), you would be destined for at least one of the Brahma realms with incredibly long lifespans, where beings feed on joy to sustain themselves. Or you may go even higher into one of the four arūpa realms where there is only mind, no tasting or touching. They're exclusively mental realms with no physical body. In these realms, it is said that lifespans are measured with a "1" followed by miles of zeros. So, they are very long.

If for some reason you have only attained the Path knowledge and haven't broken precepts, but you did not continue your meditation in this lifetime, the suttas say you will attain the Fruition on or before your death. Most of the time it will come a lot sooner.

On a retreat, Fruition could come in only a few days, or even hours, if you continue to practice without a break. Recently, a man in Chicago experienced the Path at lunchtime, and the Fruition arose for him at 1:20 a.m that night. He didn't see the links the first time, but with the Fruition he did report them.

All the higher paths are attained by just continuing the practice in the same way. There will be deeper and more subtle fetters to see and abandon. Your meditation will be easier but still, the balance of the remaining fetters will continue to arise. Now your confidence will be very strong, and you will be without doubt.

The suttas also describe another way of becoming a Sotāpanna. Simply hearing a passage of text can bring about the Sotāpanna or Sakadāgāmī Paths. In one translation, *sota* means "ear, " and *panna* means "wisdom" — wisdom through hearing. This is rare, but it did happen for many of the Buddha's disciples, like Sāriputta and Moggallāna. But for this to happen, the teacher must say exactly the right thing, and the student must be ready. Again, this is a very rare occurrence. And it tends to take a Buddha to accomplish it.

Now you have had the first two experiences of Nibbāna and have become a Sotāpanna with fruition! This is the goal of the 8 jhānas and the path I have been describing.

You have become a Noble one, one who has now broken out of the Samsaric wheel of existences — but there is still more to do. There are the Four levels of Noble ones and three more I will describe below that you still must go through to fully eliminate all craving in your mind if you want to accomplish all of this in one lifetime.

Chapter Sixteen: 2nd Stage — Sakadāgāmī

—Meditation Instruction:

Now that you have attained the first path and fruition of Sotāpanna how do you continue? That is easy — just keep doing what you are doing. Each stage of awakening is just one more step on the ladder to eliminating craving. Now the meditator spends two minutes in each direction radiating equanimity and then all around as before. And again, when the feeling fades away you observe the quiet clear mind and 6R any phenomena that arise. That's it — just keep going. And this is the process all the way to the highest attainment.

The second stage of awakening is a continued deepening of the meditation practice. You become a Sakadāgāmī when you see the links of dependent origination arising and passing away twice versus only one time for the Sotāpanna. There is a cessation, and you quickly see the twelve links of dependent origination one time, and then they arise and pass away a second time, right after the first. In total 24 links arise and pass away all at once, like train cars one after the other. This seeing of the links is followed by a moment of relief. This is not just based on the sutta texts but has been observed in student's experiences.

After you attain Sakadāgāmī Path (Magga), the Sakadāgāmī Fruition (Phala) comes when you once again experience cessation and the links of dependent origination arising and passing away twice. Sometimes in the Path experience, the student does not actually see the "bubbles," which are the links, but they will see them at the fruition.

As before, it is at Fruition where the personality changes permanently. "Path" Knowledge means really you are just on the path to the Fruit or completion of the Sakadāgāmī Stage.

At this stage, you weaken but don't fully eliminate, the fetters of:

1. *Kāma-rāga*: sensuous craving or lust.

2. *Vyāpāda*: ill-will, hatred, anger, aversion, and fear.

These have been loosened. At times, these unwholesome states will still arise if the circumstance presents itself. You will tend to avoid anger and lust, seeing them as coarse states. If they arise, you will know to 6R them; you will be surprised if they hang around very long. You will be motivated to continue your meditation to fully eliminate these disturbing states of mind. But they will still be present, just not as strong.

It is at the Fruition there is a strong release and letting go of sensual desires. This doesn't necessarily mean sexual desire but the coarse desires for sensual pleasures like entertainment, eating out, and bodily pleasure. Sexual desire is deeper and is let go later.

A note here is that if the Fruition of any path is not experienced in this lifetime, it will happen upon your death.

As a Sakadāgāmī you will have no more than just one time that you have to return to the Human or Higher Realms before you attain Final Parinibbāna and release from Samsāra. As a Sotāpanna it was seven.

"The quality of the sitting was much different from the first session today, this one being the final meditation of today. I began with quiet mind as object after having done the walking meditation with equanimity as the object. No preconceptions of what was to come in the meditation. Automatic 6Ring, which has become an impersonal and automatic process.

A blank occurred, and there was strong balance, but more so quality of mind itself is transformed. It's as if, and the best way I can describe it is, to use a metaphor, like the mind of an infant (wouldn't know exactly how an infant's mind works), and what I mean by that is mind is empty - empty of concepts, empty of thoughts, empty of identity, empty of sorrow, empty even of bliss. Certainly, bliss arose after the blank, but the mind is, following this meditation, totally free. There is no craving; there is no want-ing, desire, or striving to be or not be. Mind functions according to the needs of a given moment, but otherwise is utterly and pro-foundly quiet. Even the concept of being in the moment is utterly gone - who is there to be in the moment - total freedom from all ideas, notions, beliefs, thoughts. A fresh and clean slate." S.D. Cal-ifornia

Three Ways to Nibbāna

As outlined in this book, the first (and easiest) way to reach Nibbāna is through the jhāna path — what I am describing in this book. There are, however, two other ways to attain Nibbāna.

The second way is the way the Buddha's own awakening process unfolded. He went to the fourth jhāna and then: (1) he remembered his past lives; (2) he visited other realms and saw how and why beings were reborn there; and finally, (3) he saw how *kamma* works, how causes create more causes, in a never-ending wheel that leads to old age and death. Disenchantment and dispassion arose through this knowledge, and Nibbāna was attained. This way is called the "threefold knowledge" or *tevijja*. That is (1) knowledge of past lives, (2) knowledge of beings in other realms, and (3) knowledge of the destruction of the taints — Nibbāna.

The third way is through attaining all the psychic powers or *iddhis* and then attaining Nibbāna. This practice is most suited to people who are sensitive to feeling or emotionally driven. Being sensitive to feeling means you are a *feeling* type person who is governed by your "heart." The other type of person is an intellectual person ruled by logic and pragmatic decisions. They are best suited to go through the jhānas. People who are mixed may take the Buddha's path of the three-fold-knowledge or go through the jhānas. You can be taught to remember your past lives, but we will not go into this practice here. You can ask the teacher if it would be helpful, and they can decide whether they will teach it to you based on your progress and your personality type.

The psychic power route is a difficult path and can take many years. It brings with it the danger of becoming attached to these powers and not wanting to proceed. It can bring up a lot of conceit and arrogance about having such unique abilities. In the opinion of the Bhante Vimalaraṁsi, it is the most difficult of the ways. He says you can learn this, but it will take you ten years, and you will have to stay with him for that whole time!

Chapter Seventeen: 3rd Stage —
Anāgāmī

The Buddha considered the first and second stage of attainments to be "learner" states. The fruit of the meditation starts to develop at the next stage of Anāgāmī, where hatred and sensual desire are eliminated together with the previous three taints that were eliminated at Sotāpanna. These are the five lower fetters. This is truly a worthy and elevated state of being. Arahant, which is the fourth and final stage, then eliminates the rest of the ten fetters, completely.

To attain the higher paths of Anāgāmī and Arahant, one must practice meditation. Whereas before one might have become awakened to the first two paths just by listening to a phrase, it will now require intense meditation practice with full passage through the jhānas. Deep meditation is needed to see even more clearly the nature of the links of dependent origination and how mind is working, taking everything personally.

After more meditation and devotion to the practice, you will experience cessation again. Then you will see the links of dependent origination arise and pass away *three* times after a cessation moment in quick succession. This is the Anāgāmī Magga or Path knowledge of the third stage of awakening. After you experience Anāgāmī Magga, if you experience the same thing again, then Anāgāmī Phala or Fruition knowledge will arise three times.

An Anāgāmī has very strong equanimity. Nothing disturbs you except sometimes some restlessness that arises. Whereas before you might have reacted with some sensual desire, lust, hatred, or aversion, this is no longer the case. In addition, there isn't the slightest fear now because of the elimination of hatred. Fear is part of hatred.

You will have destroyed the first five fetters completely:

1. *Sakkāya-diṭṭhi*: personality belief in an "I" or personal self or soul.

2. *Vicikicchā*: skeptical doubt that the Dhamma is the true way.

3. *Sīlabbataparāmāsa*: clinging to rites and rituals.

4. *Kāma-rāga*: sensual craving; lust.

5. *Vyāpāda*: ill-will, hatred, anger, aversion, and fear.

Now you are very balanced in mind. This is not some super-conscious state, but simply the removal of most of the craving (*taṇhā*) from your mind. You are still you, and you still have your personality, but the influences of the craving, neurotic, fearful self are not there now.

You can continue working at your job and be in the world. Work that is involved in honest, ethical pursuits will appeal to you. You will be completely truthful and fair in your dealings with your customers and fellow employees. You will treat your fellow employees with kindness and not be shaken by any outbursts from the boss.

You will notice that you are no longer bothered by the petty fears and hang-ups that most people experience. You will become a better employee and a better boss. You will have no fear of anything and never be intimidated. You will follow directions perfectly but have no problem with pushing back against unwise orders given to you and will not fear to talk to the boss in an even, unemotional way.

You won't complain or gossip with other employees about what is wrong, and you might even be promoted up the ranks. Truly, worldly success will come as you achieve deep spiritual success.

Romantic interest is removed in a major way at the Path knowledge and eliminated entirely at the Fruition knowledge for

Anāgāmī. You will no longer desire marriage or a family. However, if you currently are married or have a family, your romantic lust will be replaced with strong, pure loving-kindness. You will live with your mate as best friends or brother and sister. You won't have any more children because your desire for sex will be lost. You will be the most wonderful parent conceivable. You won't ever get mad. And you will always love, and make plenty of time for your child. Your two-year-old won't get on your nerves anymore because you know that's the nature of a two-year-old. It's okay!

You will acquire what you need and not what you want. You won't have big desires to do things other than being happy with what you have and what you are doing right now.

You will want to share what you have learned in your meditation by teaching, but you won't be attached to promoting anything. If it happens, it happens. Your happiness with what you have achieved will be something you naturally want to share with others.

If you are working, gradually you will move away from just doing a job to make money, to looking for ways to help people directly by starting a meditation group or teaching meditation full time.

People will ask you what depression is or what suffering is, and you will be able to tell them, with no doubts. You will know how your mind works and will be able to explain it to others.

And best of all, going to the dentist won't bother you...

You will never be born again in the sensuous realms. If you don't attain Arahant in this lifetime, you will be reborn in one of the five high Brahma realms called the Pure Abodes where there are only other Anāgāmīs and Arahants. From this realm, you are destined to attained Arahanathip and get off the wheel.

But there is still more to do. There are ten fetters, and you have removed five. There are yet five more; these are the final obstacles to full awakening and freedom from even a wisp of craving.

Chapter Eighteen: 4th Stage — Arahant

When you become an Arahant, there is nothing more that can disturb your mind. You will experience *Arahatta Magga* and *Arahatta Phala* (Path and Fruition). With each Path and each Fruition experience, you will witness the arising and passing away of the links of dependent origination *four* times very quickly.

You will now have completely let go of all ten fetters of being; there is no further mental suffering for you of any kind:

1. *Sakkāya-diṭṭhi*: personality belief in an "I" or personal self or soul; the realization of the total impersonality of all existence.

2. *Vicikicchā*: skeptical doubt that the correct practice of Right Effort is the true way to awakening.

3. *Sīlabbataparāmāsa*: Realizing that rites and rituals by themselves do not lead to awakening.

4. *Kāma-rāga*: Craving for sensual pleasures.

5. *Vyāpāda*: ill-will, hatred, and fear.

6. *Rūpa-rāga and Arūpa-rāga*: the desire for material and immaterial existence. The desire to be reborn in any realm of existence. (This fetter listing has these two desires for existence combined into one, which is different from the way they are normally listed.[6])

---

[6] Ven. Bhante Vimalaraṁsi has combined the two fetters — rūpa and arūpa desires for existence — and then adds sloth and torpor as a fetter as it is defined in the suttas.

7. *Māna*: conceit, comparing with somebody else. Thinking in your mind, "I am better than you" or "I am less than you" — comparing yourself to others.

8. *Thīna-Middha*: Sloth and Torpor — Although sloth and torpor are frequently not classically included as part of the fetters, sloth and torpor are considered as one of the hindrances, which is why Bhante Vimalaraṁsi adds it here. The suttas list this as a hindrance quite clearly.

9. *Uddhacca*: Restlessness and worry.

10. *Avijjā*: Ignorance of the four noble truths and the workings of dependent origination.

You will be sought out for your wisdom, as there is no craving left in your mind and your mind is completely transparent. You see how your mind works and can easily explain it to others.

The Buddha was an Arahant and passed through all of the jhānas and went through all the stages of awakening. It is said you could ask the Buddha a question and he would give you the perfect answer. He always said exactly what was called for at the time. You may not have that depth of his understanding, or ability to speak, but it will be close. You will have experienced Nibbāna the same number of times, but your understanding of what you saw or your ability to explain it may be less.

The difference between a Buddha and an Arahant is that the Buddha has gone through countless lifetimes of purification and can be compared to a bottle that is completely empty, clear, and sparkling — there will be no taint or smell of what was there before. In an Arahant, there may be just a whiff of the personality that was there before, like a milk bottle that is emptied and cleaned out but with some faint remnant of what was there. Nonetheless, both a Buddha and an Arahant are both empty of craving and ego. Both have the same attainments.

Another difference here is that a Buddha comes to wisdom solely through their own efforts, while an Arahant reaches awakening by hearing the teachings of a Buddha.

When somebody asks you if you have any attachments to relatives or family you will say no. There is nothing that makes your mind lose its balance.

Yet, Arahants are not automatons. The Buddha was hardly an automaton. He not only responded to people who needed his help but went from place to place finding beings with "little dust in their eyes" who he felt could understand his teachings.

 He initiated conversations, seeking out beings that he could help awaken. He invited other teachers to come and argue their views with him in order to teach more students and convince more people he knew the true way. It was said that he taught the Devas and beings in other realms while everyone else was asleep at night.

You will compassionately take care of any problem that you find. You will always help others to overcome problems, but will never push your help on them. You will be equally compassionate to all beings and not just members of your family. Your loving-kindness now knows no bounds or limits. You will treat the lowly ant as well as you treat your closest friend.

You will not proselytize about Buddhism. You will answer questions and bring up Dhamma at the right time. It is unlikely anyone would ever know about your attainment, as there is no longer conceit or desire to say you are better than anyone. And as far as you are concerned, your mind is simply clear, and that is all.

There may arise in you some psychic powers, like reading minds or something else, but it just depends on your past karmic actions. Sāriputta had little in the way of powers, yet he was an intellectual giant and called "the General of the Dhamma." Moggallāna had every power that was possible, and then some. But his intellect was not as sharp, as he had more of a feeling or emotional type of personality.

Feeling personalities have a strong tendency to be able to develop psychic powers.

Your intuition about things will be exquisite. Your meditation practice will be very deep, with no distractions. You can decide to go into a jhāna, or even cessation (*Nirodha*) itself at will. You will be able to resolve to sit in the cessation of perception, feeling, and consciousness for up to seven days — if you go any longer than that your body will lose its heat and vitality and die, you must be careful.

Going into a state of extended cessation is of great benefit because, when you come out of this state, your mind will be extremely energetic and awake. You will need much less sleep. The Buddha was said to have slept only an hour per night.

People with the fruition of Anāgāmī also have a limited ability to go into cessation, and there are now students that can make this determination and sit in cessation for as long as they wish. Theoretically, based on the suttas, you can sit for seven full days, and get up as if you had just recently sat down, with no pain, full of energy.

This cessation state is different than what is mentioned in the suttas as "he attained to the cessation of perception, feeling and consciousness and his taints were destroyed by seeing with wisdom." When this state is attained you do not see the links arise and attain Nibbāna. It is simply a stilling and stopping of mind. Why one doesn't see the links again and attain Nibbāna again, I cannot say. All we can say is that there is a cessation and there is a *cessation*… different in some way.

There is also a difference between the cessation state of an Anāgāmī versus an Arahant. Cessation or in pāli, *nirodha*, is a stopping of the mental stream. Just like when you turn the water off from the faucet, and it drips a little bit and then stops, there is no more water. Nirodha is the stopping of all mental activity. It is when mind becomes so tranquil that it just stops.

However, the Arahant's mind is so pure that when he determines to go into this cessation experience, it is a state closer to Nibbāna, an unconditioned state. It is not just a stopping but something else. Instead of the conditioned mind stopping, mind now moves toward the unconditioned. Bhikkhu Ñāṇananda in his series "The Mind Stilled" in sermon sixteen, goes into this subject and calls this state by its pāli name *arahattaphalasamādhi*. He explains it here:

But the awakening in Nibbāna is not of such a temporary character. Why? Because all the influxes that lead one into the samsāric slumber with its dreams of recurrent births are made extinct in the light of that perfect knowledge of realization. That is why the term āsavakkhaya, extinction of influxes, is used in the discourses as an epithet of Nibbāna. The arahants accomplish this feat in the concentration on the fruit of arahant-hood, <u>arahattaphalasamādhi</u>.[xv]

Bhante Vimalaramsi has traveled the world and talked to and studied under many of the recognized meditation masters of our time. He is inevitably asked if he has met any Arahants. What about Venerable so and so… fill in the blank. He says, no, so far he has not met anyone that he felt was an arahant. He says you need to spend time evaluating someone to be sure they have no more fetters. But he is hopeful that we will have one soon!

You are at the end of the eight-fold path. You have eliminated Ignorance and Craving through thoroughly understanding the Four Noble Truths. You have traveled the eightfold path to the end of suffering. You will live out your current life but will not be born again to the maelstrom of samsāra and will not be subject to its *dis-ease*. You have found freedom. You have become another noble one in the Buddha's dispensation.

MN: 21. "Monks, rightly speaking, were it to be said of anyone: 'He has attained mastery and perfection in noble virtue, attained mastery and perfection in noble collectedness, attained mastery and perfection in noble wisdom, attained mastery and perfection in noble deliverance,' it is of Sāriputta indeed that rightly speaking this should be said.

22. "Monks, rightly speaking, were it to be said of anyone: 'He is the son of the Blessed One, born of his breast, born of his mouth, born of the Dhamma, created by the Dhamma, an heir in the Dhamma, not an heir in material things,' it is of Sāriputta indeed that rightly speaking this should be said.

23. "Monks, the matchless Wheel of the Dhamma set rolling by the Tathāgata is kept rolling rightly by Sāriputta."

That is what the Blessed One said. The monks were satisfied and delighted in the Blessed One's words.

"In a bhikkhu whose taints are destroyed, these [lust, hatred, delusion] are abandoned, cut off at the root, made like a palm stump, done away with so that they are no longer subject to future arising." xvi

Chapter Nineteen –
The Power of Jhāna

Experiencing the state of jhāna in this lifetime is a very powerful and far-reaching event that you can achieve – pretty quickly – *in this lifetime*. In fact, it is only second to attaining Nibbāna itself.

So, what follows is my own interpretation of..mostly Anguttara Nikaya sutta texts. Not everyone will agree with it but I think it's interesting to consider the possiblities. None of this is important for your practice, here and now, but we can speculate about the meaning.

Why is jhāna so important? It is important because that when you attain even *one moment* of jhāna, the suttas say, that if you keep your precepts and continue to lead a relatively moral life until your death, you will be destined, at a minimum, to be reborn into a realm called a Brahmaloka. This is a very high heavenly realm that corresponds to the last and highest jhāna you have attained in your practice.

For example, if the last and highest jhāna you experienced during your lifetime was the third jhāna, then you would be reborn into the third jhāna realm or brahmaloka. At the highest state/degree in this realm, it is called the Devas of Refulgent Glory (subhakinna deva).

Because of the great merit or wholesome energy of the jhāna, you will never return to a human or the lower heaven realms, much less hell, ghosts or animal realms.

Now, if that isn't good news, then there is an even more interesting fact that the suttas describe and is found in the Anguttara Nikāya. You will *attain Nibbāna* there, in that realm, without *any* return to a lower realm! Not only are you reborn into a Brahmaloka, but you never take rebirth in *any* lower realm — even if you have *not* attained Nibbāna! And all it took was to experience jhāna just once. This should motivate you to go sit!

It is widely written in most books on Buddhism that should you attain Sotāpanna, or higher attainment, that you will return, at most, seven times to any realm, before attaining final Nibbāna or Arahantship. But it can actually only be as little as one time if you attained Nibbāna *through the jhāna practice,* (note: this is the tranquil aware jhāna state we are talking about.) You will be only reborn one time in the highest jhāna realm that you experienced and attain final awakening there. There are sutta references to support this coming up, but first, we must address a common misconception that you must actually be in the state of jhāna, while you are dying, to be reborn into that higher realm.

Attaining Jhāna Just One Time

The suttas do say that if you attain a jhāna, then you are automatically reborn into the corresponding Brahmaloka realm, and never return back to a lower realm. However, most people think that when you die you have to be in the state of jhāna.

The thought is that if you attain the first jhāna, then rebirth is in the first jhāna realm. Rebirth is very pleasant and is one Aeon long there. If you attain the 2nd jhāna, then this realm is higher still, and so on up to the 8th level of the Arupā base of neither-perception-nor-non-perception.

I'll use the below sutta — it is a suttacentral.net translation, but I am going to change some of the [text] to Bhikkhu Bodhi's version. This becomes clearer with his Anguttara Nikāya translation, printed by Wisdom Publications, in 2012, on page 507. This is a sutta entitled "Goodwill [Loving-kindness]," the book of fours, Sutta 125.

This is to address the skeptics that think that to be reborn in a Brahmaloka requires that you *be in that jhāna meditation state* at the moment of your death.

Anguttara Nikāya 125 (5), Book of Fours, "Loving-Kindness"

"Monks, there are these four types of individuals to be found exist-
ing in the world. Which four?

"There is the case where an individual keeps pervading the first di-
rection—as well as the second direction, the third, & the fourth—
with an awareness imbued with loving-kindness or Mettā. Thus,
he keeps pervading above, below, & all around, everywhere & in
every respect the all-encompassing cosmos with an awareness im-
bued with good will [loving-kindness]: abundant, expansive, im-
measurable, free from hostility, free from ill will. He savors that,
longs for that, finds satisfaction through that. Staying there—fixed
on that, dwelling there often, not falling away from that [D]-easily
able to return to that jhāna]—then when he dies, he reappears in
conjunction with the devas of Brahma's retinue. [First Jhāna
Realm] The devas of Brahma's retinue, monks, have a life-span of
an eon."

If we look at the sutta, this idea of having to be in the jhāna state
at death appears not to be the case — *luckily*. You only need to be able
to experience in the time period that is near your death, through a
normal sitting, the ability to get back into that jhāna again. With this
condition, you have fulfilled the criteria.

The only exception would be if you had committed any of the *five*
heinous crimes: killing an Arahant; killing your Mother or Father;
causing a schism in the Sangha, or wounding a Buddha – all of which
are either impossible or extremely unlikely. As long you meet these
criteria you will be reborn into, for example, that very pleasant first
jhāna realm.

And if you are able to attain the first jhāna in the time period
around your death, then you will be assured of being reborn into
that realm. It doesn't say you have to be in the jhāna at the
moment of death. Who could actually accomplish that anyway?
You are dying! You may be sick and weak. It would take a Buddha,

but then he is already fully enlightened, and it would not apply to him, anyway.

Most meditator TWIM students would likely be able to get into a jhāna, easily enough, later on in life if they have kept their practice up, or at least led a moral life and kept precepts. It's like getting on a bike…

The next part is now subject to more interpretation, and I will do my best to help with this. The sutta says that whatever jhāna realm that you are reborn into, having arrived in that realm by your jhāna practice, you will attain Nibbāna in that realm, never to return to any lower realm, or for that matter any realm at all. But it starts off with saying that someone, other than the Buddha's disciples, will go to the lower realms immediately after having enjoyed that high rebirth.

Continued: *Aṅguttara Nikāya 125 (5), Book of Fours, "Loving-Kindness"*

"A run-of-the-mill [Worldling] person having stayed there, having used up all the life-span of those devas, goes to hell, to the animal womb, to the state of the hungry shades (ghosts). But a disciple of the Blessed One [below it says Noble disciple, so this means following the Buddha's training in the aware jhānas – not concentration jhānas!], having stayed there, having used up all the life-span of those devas, is unbound [attains Final Nibbāna] right in that state of being. This, monks, is the difference, this the distinction, this the distinguishing factor, between an educated disciple of the noble ones [those having practiced the jhāna path that the Buddha found] and an uneducated run of the mill person [a disciple of another system of meditation, like absorption concentration (the Buddha tried them all before finding the Aware Jhāna Path)], when there is future destination and rebirth."

The sutta implies that if you attain jhāna and you have learned true meditation practice from the *Buddha,* then you will be reborn into the jhāna realm, and attain final Nibbāna in that realm and get off the wheel right there, with no further births.

However, there is this quite ominous warning — and believe me, most people will not like this at all – about your subsequent rebirth after having been reborn into a jhāna realm if you did *not* learn your meditation from the Buddha.

If you attain jhāna using concentration methods taught by other teachers, (The Buddha he rejected concentration methods, early on in his search) you will indeed, be reborn to this Brahmaloka and live out your life there but, shockingly, you will not gracefully fall down from that Brahmaloka to a deva or heavenly realm, and then gently are reborn into a human birth, as your good kamma and merit is used up, but, rather, fall *directly* into the lower planes of existence like the animal or hell realms.

This does not agree with the Abhidhamma, which most monks would consult for this type of inquiry. In fact, there is disagreement about whether the Abhidhamma was spoken by the Buddha at all. It is generally theorized by many scholars that it was added to the basket of texts at the 3rd council of monks, some 200 years after the Buddha died. So, how could he have said this?

So, if we go by the suttas only, then we need to change our views. After explaining this sutta to one of our more advanced students in the USA, he said he did recall one of his past lives in a Brahmaloka heaven realm, and he remembered actually dying from that realm. He was shocked to find he had fallen all the way down to become an animal in his next rebirth – from a god to a dog!

A Sri Lankan student, at Dhamma Sukha for a retreat, agreed with this idea and quoted a sutta reference (I don't recall now) where the Buddha is asked about a stream of ants walking on the ground. He said that these beings had fallen from a Brahmaloka (!) and had not gotten off the wheel and attained Nibbāna. The Buddha pointed this out, as an admonishment to Sariputta, who had just gotten someone. on their death bed, into a wholesome enough state for rebirth, after death, into a heavenly deva realm. The admonishment was for *only* getting them into a *heavenly realm* and not giving them enough wisdom for them to attain the knowledge of Nibbāna right there and get off the wheel either this or only one more lifetime.

If you attain a few absorption-concentration jhānas then, eventually, that karma runs out – and it really runs out! You might become an *ant* after your stay in a heavenly palace!

I'll note here, that I believe the above example may be a student that only attained the Brahmaloka through an act of good merit, not attaining any jhānas, but only was listening to Sariputta and through their "giving ear," their mind became elevated enough to get into a Brahmaloka through the hearing of a sutta. Because it was not through jhāna practice, there would be no protection from falling from that realm.

There are stories of people acquiring enough merit at the time of the Buddha to be reborn, even as high as the Brahmalokas, but due to not having any jhāna practice to protect them, either concentration or tranquil aware jhāna, they fell directly to the lower realms, as that was the only good merit keeping them in the higher realm. I don't know. All this is speculation. But let's go to the sutta:

Pg. 347 Imperturbable 116(4) -Anguttara Nikāya BB 2012

*"Monks, there are three types of persons found in this world." 1) Here, monks with the attainment of the base of infinite space...this person relishes it and finds satisfaction in it. If he is firm in...and has not lost it when he dies, he is reborn in companionship with the devas of the infinite space. The lifespan is 20,000 Aeons. This worldling remains there all his life, and when he has completed the entire lifespan of those devas, **he goes down to hell**, to the animal realm or to the sphere of afflicted spirits.*

But, the Blessed one's disciple remains there all his life, and when he has completed his entire lifespan of those devas, <u>he attains Nibbāna in that very same state of existence</u>." [This is the difference between the instructed noble one's disciple and the worldling.]

The sutta goes on to repeat for the Base of Infinite Consciousness and Nothingness.

So, this is saying that if you are able to enter into a jhāna - in this specific case an arupā jhāna at death - *and* you have arrived at this realm through wrong concentration – then you are liable to fall, quite sharply, from that realm, directly into a lower realm, without gradually falling first into a deva realm and then, again further, down to a human realm.

This doesn't say a "Noble Disciple," it says the Blessed one's disciple. Just a disciple is all. This means they are someone following the jhāna practice path laid out by the Buddha. They don't have any attainments as if they did they would be referred to as a *noble disciple*.

In summary, I leave you with some quotes from the suttas to suggest (it is up to the reader to decide) that if you keep up your meditation practice and are able to get into a jhāna near and around the time of your death, then you will not only be reborn into the corresponding Brahmaloka but *attain Nibbāna there*, without ever returning to a lower rebirth. Pretty good!

Again, this is commonly thought as only the domain of the stream-enterer or a higher noble disciple. It was thought that you had to have the 3rd stage Nibbāna experience to never return to this world or lower — in fact, all you need to do is just ***attain a jhāna!*** This is a wonderful discovery, and if true, we are very lucky — even for those whose practice is only a little bit advanced, with just the first jhāna attained.

That said, the Buddha always admonished followers not ever to stop and to continue the practice until final awakening was achieved, here and now. He had high expectations and demanded the highest achievement. Either you were an Arahant, or you were still a rookie…

Jhānānāgāmī or Jhānānāgāmītā

Reading through the Anguttara Nikāya is quite interesting as there are some nuggets in these texts that don't appear elsewhere in the other Nikāyas. What I found, specifically, is a different understanding, or definition of the *Sotāpanna* and *Sakadāgāmī* Noble Disciples – 1st and 2nd level attainments.

It is thought that only an Anāgāmī attainment (3rd stage of awakening) will give you enough merit, for your rebirth in your next lifetime to be reborn in a Brahmaloka — and in the case of the Anāgāmī, a very special Brahmaloka called the *Pure Abodes,* where only Anāgāmīs are reborn because they have eliminated the first five fetters of craving. From there, they attain Arahantship in that realm and are never take birth again.

It is an incredible accomplishment for this to be your last lifetime in the lower realms — even the human and Deva realms — and this is what the Anāgāmī achieves.

However, I found some good news for the first two lower Noble levels. In the Anguttara Nikāya, for the first two noble disciples, if you attain Sotāpanna or Sakadāgāmī, *and* you did this through the *jhāna* meditation practice, then you may be reborn *into the Brahmalokas* never to return — like the Anāgāmī!

The 1st and 2nd paths can be attained through hearing a sutta; however, when you attain them with jhāna practice, your advantage is that you are reborn into the highest realm available to a meditator. You will *not* return to any lower realm. You will attain Nibbāna in that realm and get off the wheel right there. No more lifetimes, like seven lives for a Sotāpanna, and one for a Sakadāgāmī, which is the case described in so many commentaries.

Those Noble disciples that have the attainment of Sotāpanna or Sakadāgāmī that was attained through the jhāna practice are given the unique title of **Jhānānāgāmī** or **Jhānānāgāmītā** per Bhikkhu Bodhi's notes (from a commentary he does note) in his translation of the Anguttara Nikāya: notes #539 and #2193 which I reproduce later.

Let's go to the suttas: Here is a partial sutta quote regarding the never-returner status of Sotāpanna or Sakadāgāmī:

Pg. 1541 "The Deed-Born Body" 219(9) AN

"...This noble disciple understands...when the liberation of mind by loving-kindness has been developed in this way [who has attained the jhānas through the Brahmavihāras], it leads to <u>non-returning</u> for a wise bhikkhu here who does not penetrate to a further liberation.

A similar sutta is found on pg. 327 "Autumn" 94(3) AN

"Bhikkhus, just as, in the autumn, when the sky is clear and cloudless, the sun, ascending in the sky, dispels all darkness from space as it shines and beams and radiates, so too, when the dust-free, stainless Dhamma-eye arises in the noble disciple, together with the arising of vision, the noble disciple abandons three fetters: person-existence view, doubt, and wrong grasp of behavior and observances.

"Afterward, when he departs from two states, longing, and ill will, then secluded from sensual pleasures, secluded from unwholesome states, he enters and dwells in the first jhāna, which consists of rapture and pleasure born of seclusion, accompanied by thought and examination. If bhikkhus, the noble disciple should pass away on that occasion, there is no fetter bound by which he might return to this world."

The above person clearly becomes free of three fetters and has become a Sotāpanna. Bhikkhu Bodhi explains in a note #539, Page 1663, relating to the above passage, he calls this type of individual a Jhānānāgāmī or as in the duplicate note #2193: a Jhānānāgāmītā.

Here is the note: #2193, Page. 1859 by Bhikkhu Bodhi

"This phrase normally denotes the attainment of non-returning. Mp (Commentaries), however, identifies this disciple as a "jhāna non-returner," Jhānānāgāmītā , that is a stream-enterer or once-returner who also attains jhāna. Though such a practitioner has

not yet eliminated the two fetters of sensual desire and ill-will, by attaining jhāna, he or she is bound to be reborn in the form realm and attain nibbāna there, without taking another rebirth in the sense sphere."

The difference between the two types of "jhānānagāmīs" is the first is male and the other female.

So, now we have a new type of "Noble One;" one that has attained Sotāpanna and Sakadāgāmī, attained by following the jhāna meditation system — not attained through listening to a phrase or other method. He/she has earned the achievement of not having to be born again in the lower Deva or Human realms and will be reborn in a Brahmaloka and attain Final Nibbāna there.

It says the *form realm*, and I would theorize that this is the Pure Abodes, as this is the <u>highest</u> form realm. Otherwise, logically, if you do attain to the arupā jhānas, which you would do practicing by using the jhāna path, then you would be reborn in the higher arupā or mental Brahmalokas where there is only mind, ie. The base of nothingness etc. This would not be a birth in a form realm, but rather, a *formless* realm.

This seems fairly logical as it would make no sense for someone who attained Sotāpanna to be reborn again as a human being with the same people they grew up with — the same high school dance party that they went to; the same people who never knew or followed precepts. No, I don't think that makes sense. A Sotāpanna is a very high being, called a Saint in many places, and it would be very doubtful that he/she would be reborn into the company of worldlings. Even reborn as a regular monk among monks who, themselves, are still worldlings. Many monks these days are "study monks" or serve laypeople performing rites and rituals and have not meditated.

I will leave you with all these ideas here in the last chapter to contemplate, but I found it rather interesting and hopeful. It may be quite confusing, but I seem to have become a true "Buddhist Geek," as I am interested in the finer (perhaps really, really finer) points of attainments. This research, of course, is solely based on what the suttas say, which I would hope to be true and correct! The interpretation, of course, is just my own.

Chapter Twenty — After the Retreat

People ask after a retreat, or what they think is a major attainment, "Now what do I do?" How do I practice each day.

First, one of the misunderstandings is that you will be able to "dial up" the last jhāna you attained, or for that matter, any jhāna, at will. No, you won't be able to do that. Your practice will take a dip and the mind will sink back into a coarser state. Daily life brings stresses, both physical and emotional. These will wear you out and will affect your meditation. All of the news, social media and, relationships you have, will make your mind more restless and agitated. So your meditation will be restless one day and groggy the next. Sometimes you will just be frazzled!

It doesn't matter, you just continue your practice each day, as long as you can. Bhante Vimalaramsi suggests if you want good progress each day you will sit and walk for a total of two hours or more. Most people will not have that time to spend but can sit 30 minutes or an hour each day. So do that! Get up a little earlier to sit. Progress will continue, albeit slower. Every day the more pure mind states you bring up, the more mental merit and purity you obtain.

It is suggested that you get up in the morning and go through your morning things like a bath and having breakfast and then sit. Sitting right away when you get up may lead to sleepiness.

If you were working with a spiritual friend as your object of meditation, then continue that process. When your feeling of mettā arises up into your head and ceases being in your heart or chest area, then go to the "Breaking Down the Barriers" section in this book and practice that for a day or two.

When your mind is okay with the four groups of beings, and you don't have any gross ill will, then continue on to "Radiating in the Six Directions" practice and start with radiating loving-kindness per the instructions in that section. See the fourth jhāna chapter in this book for all of the above instructions.

If you have advanced and were practicing at the formless jhāna levels of either Mettā, Karuna, Mudita or Upekkhā then *on a retreat* you would just return and work with the jhāna/feeling you were working with. However, in daily life, you would be advised to start each meditation session with mettā or lovingkindness. This is the gateway to all of the other jhānas.

Many students will get into equanimity on a retreat and experience all of the higher jhānas and, perhaps, get an attainment. They think that they simply can return to radiating equanimity during daily life – this might not be possible. If you start radiating equanimity, you may actually just be radiating a kind of calm, which is really not equanimity at all, and your practice won't get anywhere. This might leave you frustrated and wondering why nothing is happening.

Off retreat, your mind is agitated and restless, and no longer in a high state, so it is best to re-start with mettā. This loving-kindness that is radiated outward softens the mind and brings tranquility and energy/joy to your sitting. In a very short time, your mind will return to the last level you attained. Remember, the brahmavihāra practice is something that happens automatically. No need to figure this out – just start with mettā, and you will go up the chain of "vihāras."

If you are doing directions, you can do five minutes to each direction, as you did previously. If you have had an attainment you are suggested to radiate only two minutes in each direction and then all around.

Then, the rest of the day use your 6Rs to release and relax into disturbing mental states that might be triggered. Try radiating loving-kindness while you are driving or shopping. Develop wholesome states – the longer you stay in the wholesome, the deeper your practice will go...eventually!

Keep your precepts! This is very important for your practice to go further. Avoid intoxicants especially, as that might be the tougher precept to keep than the others. Peer pressure can come into play here but just wave it off. This will have significant payoffs for you in the future.

Develop your Dana or generosity. Give more to your local sangha. Give more in general. This softens the mind further *and* makes merit that *will* affect your practice positively!

And, of course, continue to sit!

The Path to Nibbāna

Chapter 21 - Review of Meditation Instructions & Stages of Progress

You may be new to Tranquil Wisdom Insight Meditation, taught by Bhante Vimalaramsi, and need a refresher on the practice and all of the signposts along the way. You may have forgotten some of the instructions on how to begin, and what to do when the meditation changes. This chapter will give you a summary of all of the instructions and many of the signs of progress. After reading the previous chapters this will summarize much of what you just read and you can come back here and refer to this, if you have forgotten some steps. The jhānas are not identified, as it is what you experience that is most important, not what jhāna you are in. For that you can check the previous chapters. This is the barebones of the entire process, all the way to Nibbāna.

BEGINNING INSTRUCTIONS – for more information go back to the detailed chapters at the beginning of the book.

- Sit for at least 30 minutes, either on a cushion or a chair. Later, a chair will be a better choice.

- Do not move for any reason. Do not itch or twitch.

- Bring up a smile on your lips, in your heart, and in your mind! Keep the smile going for the entire sitting. A little Buddha smile.

- Bring up a happy memory and *feel* that memory. See yourself holding a baby-what do you feel? Look into his/her eyes. How about playing with a dog or a bunch of puppies-what do you feel? Lovingkindness! Smile into that feeling.

- Now wish yourself this feeling of lovingkindness and stay with that. Stay with that feeling and let it seep into your being for the first 10 minutes of your sitting.

- To help you bring up the feeling of lovingkindness you may use phrases like, "May I be happy", "May I be peaceful" or others. Don't use this as a mantra, but only now and then to *nudge* along that subtle warm, glowing feeling of lovingkindness.

- If your mind wanders or is distracted from the feeling then practice the 6R process as defined in more detail elsewhere in the book. This is very important! 6Rs:

    o 1. Recognize you are distracted.

    o 2. Release your attention to the distraction.

    o 3. Relax any tension and tightness continuing to pull you to the distraction.

    o 4. Re-smile and bring up the feeling again with a smile

    o 5. Return to your object of meditation.

    o 6. Repeat/Continue and keep it going.

- The next 20 minutes of the sitting (or balance of the sitting) pick a Spiritual Friend (explained elsewhere) and radiate to and surround your friend with this warm feeling of lovingkindness that you now experience for yourself.

- During your sitting develop a content peaceful state of mind. Do not try too hard. Just *hang out* with your Friend and just feel happy to be meditating. If you notice a knot of tension in your head then you are trying too hard. Back off, and relax, and smile more. Notice the tension but accept it is there and let it be. 6R. Return to your spiritual friend. Gradually the tension will go away because you aren't feeding it with your attention anymore. All you need to do is relax and smile, and feel that smile!

BEGINNERS' PROGRESS SIGNS

- Gradually, as you <u>patiently</u> stay with yourself or your Spiritual Friend, the mind will start to calm. The first 20 minutes of your sitting will generally be active, and if you can sit through that, and don't move and smile, most of that will soon pass.
- There will come a point where all of a sudden joy (*piti*) arises. It will be something that you have never experienced. It may be extreme or moderate, but you will feel it. Then a feeling of tranquility will follow.
- After you experience this joy you should now let go of the verbal phrases that you have been using. Those phrases may actually create tension in your mind/head. Verbal phrases you have been using like "May I be happy" can be let go. You only need to remember the feeling of lovingkindness and bring that back when it weakens.

- Don't get caught in, nor suppress the joy- just acknowledge it is there and return to your object of meditation, your Spiritual Friend.
- As you continue, the joy will change and the "happy noise" in the mind will take a step down – kind of like when you are sitting and the refrigerator stops; you suddenly notice how quiet it has become.
- You will tend to have more *confidence* in the TWIM method now. You have a feeling you have found the right path. This confidence just arises on its own.
- Keep smiling and patiently stay with your Spiritual Friend. You 6R any itches or distractions. The feeling of lovingkindness will be in your heart area and lower body.
- Now, you notice that parts of your body just seem to not be there anymore. The mind has calmed a lot more. You know your hands are there… but you don't feel them. However, if there is contact or someone touches you, you will feel it. You are still aware of the outside world.
- Now the feeling will change from a more coarse joy to a more subtle feeling of happiness, or peaceful contentment (*sukha*). Equanimity starts to arise more now. A strong feeling of balance arises in the mind. You should be sitting at least 45 minutes to one hour at this stage.
- As you sit in this peaceful feeling, gradually this feeling of lovingkindness moves up into the head. Your awareness seems to change. You were feeling the body but now you are coming into more of a mental realm. You have now become an advanced meditator.

- Now, with your sitting practice, you alternate with 20-30 minutes of walking meditation. You "take your spiritual friend for a walk." Stroll at a normal pace, not slow walking, but enough to get your heart going. Keep your spiritual friend in mind. See him/her smiling and happy while sending them your wish of lovingkindness. Much progress can be attained through the walking meditation. You can *walk* into the jhānas.

ADVANCED INSTRUCTIONS AND PROGRESS

Changing your meditation instructions now

- Next: Breaking down the Barriers

Once the feeling of meditation moves up into your head, we ask you to do the *Breaking Down the Barriers* exercise. This should not take anymore than just one sitting. See Chapter 4 for instructions.

- Next: Radiating to the Six Directions

Now that you have finished your *Breaking down the Barriers* exercise, you will start to radiate your strong feeling of lovingkindness outward, like a candle, or like a lighthouse radiating warmth and heat into the six directions.

Instructions:

- First, radiate your lovingkindness feeling for five minutes to beings in front of you (you can pick the order that works for you); then all beings behind you for five minutes; then to the left, to the right, down below, and all beings above you. Five minutes in each direction. A total of 30 minutes in six directions.

- Then for the rest of the sitting (which should be in the area of 1-1.5 hours now), you radiate to all beings in *all* directions *at the same time*. You become a bubble of mettā with this feeling of pure lovingkindiness. You see this feeling seep or flow outward as you wish beings happiness. Keep your little Buddha smile with you.

Advanced Progress Signposts

- As you radiate to the directions, you feel lovingkindness (<u>Mettā</u>) going outward. It can be subtle or like a strong radiance or even a golden light. Continue – no need to do more. No need to make it stronger, if it is weak. Just whatever is there. Carefully 6R when your mind's attention wanders.

- As you feel more settled this feeling of lovingkindess will change. It gets quieter. Now, this feeling is turning into *Karuna* or Compassion. Your mind feels like it is expanding in all directions. It can be strong for some or just "feels big and expansive" for others.

- Next, this expansion pulls back in and the feeling in the mind changes to *Mudita* or a feeling of sublime Joy. You may see a flickering at one of the sense doors. It can be just that, or you may see consciousness arising and passing away like frames in a movie film, frame by frame. You may also start to experience strong insights into *anattā* or impersonality, as well as *anicca* or impermanence.

- Next, you take what's (not) happening between the frames as your new object of meditation. There is a strong Equanimity or balance (*Upekkhā*) that now arises. The feeling of Joy has changed to balance and quiet. There isn't much activity or mind-objects to notice. There is very strong stability. You should notice the balanced feeling and stay with that feeling. Now radiate *that* to the directions. This feeling of balance or equanimity is now your object of meditation.

- You will also have this perception that "there is nothing." Thoughts have stopped. The mind is quite still now. Awareness has moved fully up into the head. You don't notice your body at all. You are truly in a mental realm now. You *no longer have a body* is one way to look at it. Feeling and sensation are perceived by mind–even the feelings from the body are just in mind, right?

- There can be lights that arise. Just 6R them and come back to observing and wishing Equanimity. Always come back to the feeling. Your mind will become bright and clear. You can sit longer now–up to 2 hours. If the sitting is going well then just keep sitting! If you get up now, when it is going well, you inevitably will need to build up your mindfulness once more, in the next sitting, to get back to where you just were. Take advantage of your progress and go deeper now, not later.

- Get in some fast walking in between sittings to get your heart pumping. Sitting can slow down your energy. As you walk you should radiate Equanimity to all directions at the same time. Become a bubble moving forward radiating equanimity.

- After some time in this state, where there is nothing, your mind will fall, initially, into what seems like a dream. It is dream-like, yet you feel that you are awake. Your awareness is just barely there. You will come out of this state in a short time. The mind will now be more still than ever before. Now, we instruct you to sit with this <u>Quiet Mind</u> for up to two to three hours. Don't push or try too hard–gently! The distractions are now only just vibrations, and perhaps lights and patterns. As soon as your attention goes there, back away and relax. Just release/relax quickly is all that's needed.

- You may sit with nothing happening at all for 5 minutes or even 15 minutes. Your mind is completely unmoving, like a rock. It won't shake. If it does then 6R. Be very mindful and 6R right then.

- At this stage, the feeling of Equanimity has <u>stopped</u>. Now, '*Quiet mind*' is your object of meditation. You understand that there is no movement, you observe and just (contentedly and dispassionately) be with that. There is now some relief from the noise of the worldly-mind. Always come back to just being with understanding and knowing that you are observing *quiet mind*. If your attention wanders at all, from this present moment of peace and non-activity, then 6R quickly but softly and come back. Enjoy the peace of no activity and relax. Keep alert and mindful for vibrations and attention shifts and back away and release and relax right then.

- It may take 15 minutes, or 30 minutes, or an hour but

the mind will take a step down to a new level of quiet. "Patience leads to Nibbāna." Just continue. You may say "nothing is happening– time to stop." No! Keep going–you are making huge progress staying in this special state. At any moment the mind could take yet another step down.

Finally, after some time, the mind, all of a sudden, just stops. There can be a space or blackout, or not even that, but you feel as though you are coming back from somewhere. It is like the lights were turned off but all you know now is that they are coming back on.

- If you are aware enough, you will experience a quick feeling of Relief. Like a burden thrown off. That may only just be a moment or two. Then an upsurge of joy arising–an *all-pervading* joy in the whole body. You feel very happy!

- You have just experienced Nibbāna for the first time! For more details see chapter fourteen. Congratulations!

After Nibbāna, then what?

- Now just return to your sitting practice and continue in the same way. Usually, you can start with radiating two minutes of Equanimity to each direction, and then all around. You follow the same process over and over, all the way to Arahantship, through the four stages of sainthood. There is nothing special that you need to do other then just keep going through the stages of practice, over and over until you experience another cessation, and subsequently another moment of Nibbāna, and attain the next step in awakening.

- After the retreat, you may not be able to bring up Equanimity. That's ok. Just start with Lovingkindness again. It will always take you <u>automatically</u> all the way through the jhānas, to the goal. Mettā *is* the *Gateway* to Nibbāna.

For more information:
Dhamma Sukha Meditation Center
<u>www.dhammasukha.org</u>
www.thepathtonibbana.com

Email: david@dhammasukha.org

"*Meditate, Ānanda, do not delay, or else you will regret it later.* This is our instruction to you." That is what the Blessed One said. The venerable Ānanda was satisfied and delighted in the Blessed One's words." *xvii*

End Notes – The Path to Nibbāna

i K. Sri. Dhammananda, *The Dhammapada*, Introduction pg. XXII, WFB 2010

ii *Majjhima Nikāya* 26, "The Noble Search": section 16.

iii *Saṃyutta Nikāya*, translated by Bhikkhu Bodhi (Somerville, MA): Wisdom Publication, 2000), p. 537.

iv *Majjhima Nikāya* 36, "The Greater Discourse to Saccaka."

v http://library.dhammasukha.org/jhanas-or-no.html

vi *Practical Insight Meditation* and *Progress of Insight*, Ven. Mahāsi Sayadaw, (Kandy, Sri Lanka: Buddhist Publication Society (1971).

vii *Right Concentration – A Practical Guide to the Jhānas*, Leigh Brasington, p.46 Shambala 2015

viii *Right Concentration – A Practical Guide to the Jhānas*, Leigh Brasington p.54 Shambala 2015

ix *Majjhima Nikāya* 111, Sect 4.0, translated by Bhikkhu Bodhi (Somerville, MA): Wisdom Publication, 2000)

x Saṃyutta Nikāya, SN 54-46 Bhikkhu Bodhi, Wisdom Publications, p. 1607

xi http://library.dhammasukha.org/brahmavihara-vs-breath.html

xii http://www.dhammasukha.org/bhikkhu-nanananda.html

xiii http://www.tipitaka.net/tipitaka/dhp/verseload.php?verse=001

xiv http://www.beyondthenet.net/dhamma/nibbanaReal.htm

xv http://www.beyondthenet.net/calm/nibbana16.htm

xvi *Majjhima Nikāya* 43, Bhikkhu Bodhi, Wisdom Publications

xvii *Majjhima Nikāya* 152. Sec. 18, Bhikkhu Bodhi, Wisdom Publications

Biography

David Johnson has been in residence at Dhamma Sukha Meditation Center since 2010. He is a longtime senior student of Bhante Vimalaraṁsi and has participated in many retreats.

Currently, he is a *kappiya* (personal attendant) for Ven. Bhante Vimalaraṁsi, when he resides at the center. David also did a temporary ordination in 2012 under Bhante Vimalaramsi. He took on the robes for a short period.

History

David was a student of many Vipassanā retreats using the Mahāsi method, starting from the age of nineteen. He spent nearly twenty years taking yearly retreats. He also has completed over twelve retreats with Bhante Vimalaraṁsi and has been his student since 2006.

David has taken and accumulated video footage of and personally met Dipa Ma and Mahāsi Sayadaw. He previously meditated under Joseph Goldstein, Jack Kornfield, and U Silananda. He has brought the footage of these great teachers to the internet for all to enjoy.

David is from Bellevue, near Seattle, Washington. From 1973 to 1978, he was the meditation center retreat manager for the Stillpoint Institute, a San Jose, California-based

Vipassanā center. He assisted in the growth of the center and managed its financial and administrative affairs.

From the 1980s to 2010 he worked in the San Francisco Bay Area at several networking companies as a production and logistics manager. He then decided to join Bhante in his mission to bring TWIM to the world in 2010 and moved to Missouri permanently.

In 2015 he wrote, using Bhante Vimalaraṁsi's introductory talks and meditator experiences, the recent instruction book, A Guide to Tranquil Wisdom Meditation.

His current duties at Dhamma Sukha include:

- Serving as secretary-treasurer and board member.
- Guiding monthly online retreats since 2015 and some on-site retreats.
- Managing the retreat center.
- Maintaining the website and social media accounts.
- Book publishing all of Bhante's books.
- Producing Videos — producing all footage of Bhante found on the website and YouTube.

You can directly get in touch with David at david@dhammasukha.org or reach him through the Dhamma Sukha website.

Resources

Dhamma Sukha Meditation Center website: http://www.dhammasukha.org.

Majjhima Nikāya. Translated by Bhikkhu Bodhi. Somerville, MA: Wisdom Publications, 1995.

Kraft, Doug. *Buddha's Map: His Original Teachings on Awakening, Ease, and Insight in the Heart of Meditation.* Grass Valley, CA: Blue Dolphin Publishing, 2013.

Vimalaraṁsi, Bhante. *The Anapanasati Sutta: A Practical Guide to Mindfulness of Breathing and Tranquil Wisdom Meditation,* Carmel, NY: Buddhist Association of the USA, 2006.

Vimalaraṁsi, Bhante. *Meditation Is Life, Life Is Meditation.* Annapolis, MO: Dhamma Sukha, 2014.

Vimalaraṁsi, Bhante. *Breath of Love.* Jakarta, Indonesia: Ehipassiko Foundation, 2012.

Vimalaraṁsi, Bhante. *Moving Dhamma.* Vol. 1. Annapolis, MO: Dhamma Sukha, 2012.

Vimalaraṁsi, Bhante. *A Guide to Tranquil Wisdom Meditation (TWIM).* Annapolis, MO: Dhamma Sukha, 2016.

Orders:

Available from most online bookstores. Local bookstores can order it for you. Book Depository will ship books anywhere in the world for free!　　　www.bookdepository.com

Meditation questions welcome anytime.
Email: david@dhammasukha.org

Addendum

Guide to Forgiveness Meditation

An Effective Method to Dissolve Blocks to Loving-Kindness and Living in the Present

Bhante Vimalaramsi

Introduction

The Buddha was a meditation teacher. He taught meditation for 45 years after he became fully awakened. When you study and practice meditation, you will not be entirely successful until you master the definitions and interwoven nature of two words. Meditation and Mindfulness.   I can give you the definitions, but then you must experience for yourself how these two work together.

In the Buddhist teachings, Meditation means, 'observing the movement of mind's attention moment-to-moment, in order to see clearly how the links Dependent of Origination actually work.' Mindfulness means 'remembering to observe 'How' mind's attention moves from one thing to another. This use of mindfulness actually causes mind to become sharper as you go as you experience more subtle states of mind. It isn't hard to see why you must develop this precise mindfulness to keep the meditation going smoothly.

Many people practice Loving-Kindness meditation, but, according to a few people, the power of it doesn't seem to change much for them in their daily lives.   If it doesn't take off quite right, in the beginning, we might run into difficulty with this practice, and it can be like hitting a wall. It's good to know that there is a key to the solution for developing mettā in our daily activities. That solution is learning to smile as much as you can remember.

Apparently, in some cases, if we do get into trouble, we can clear the runway for our Mindfulness of Loving-Kindness to take off by first learning to use Mindfulness of Forgiveness meditation.   This is an extremely powerful and cleansing practice. Forgiveness is a form of loving-kindness that really clears our mind of negative or unwholesome states.

The reason this book came into being is because of the many questions teachers are asked about 'why doesn't my Mettā arise easily?'. It is because we need to forgive ourselves first before we can send out pure love to others.

CHAPTER ONE - Preparation

At times, there can be confusion about how to effectively practice this Mindfulness of Forgiveness meditation. So, this booklet is dedicated only to this meditation on forgiveness so you can begin the practice with a clear goal and better understanding.

When people are practicing Loving-Kindness Meditation, you might run into a barrier as you try to send out Loving-Kindness to yourself and others. If this happens after a few days, and you are not successful in feeling the mettā in the retreat, it may be suggested for you to take a step back and start doing the Forgiveness Meditation to overcome these blocks. After all, we cannot sincerely send Loving-kindness and Forgiveness to someone else when we do not have it for ourselves. This practice is not just used for a person pursuing Loving-Kindness and Compassion meditation. Any person can make the commitment to clean house by doing this forgiveness work. After this is done for the first time, one feels many years younger, because oftentimes, a great weight has been lifted off your heart and mind.

Some people have the idea that this meditation is a completely different kind of meditation from the Loving-Kindness meditation. That is not so. It should be made clear from the beginning that the Forgiveness Meditation is not outside of the development of Loving-Kindness and is a part of mettā. For anyone who has difficulty in feeling loving-kindness, this can be the first step. It creates a firm bridge between heart and mind that is then used to help all other kinds of meditation succeed. It is a cleansing for the heart: another opening of the heart we can add to our initial practice of Generosity.

In truth, this meditation is probably the most powerful meditation that I know. It can clear away mental blocks that pop up from old attachments or dislikes towards various people, or events that happened to you in your past life experiences. If you follow directions closely, and you are patient when you practice, then pain and suffering will gradually dissolve any hard-heartedness you still carry in your mind, about past life wounds.

When you practice Forgiveness meditation, all of the basic rules will remain the same. You still sit in a reasonably quiet space to do this work. Be sure you are wearing loose, comfortable clothing. Sit in a comfortable position, on the floor or in a chair. If you do use a chair, don't lean into the back of the chair. Sit with your spine nicely straight but not tightly erect. Sit in a position that does not bring up physical pain in general for you. You should follow the basics of practicing Right Effort using Tranquil Wisdom Insight Meditation (TWIM).

When you practice, sit for a minimum of 30 minutes each time. Sit longer if things are going smoothly and you have the time. At whatever time you decide to break your sitting, stand up slowly. Keep your observation going as you stand up. Stretch slowly if desired.

While you are sitting, do not move at all. Don't wiggle your toes, don't scratch. If your body needs to cough or sneeze, do not hold this in; just sneeze or cough! Keep some tissues close by for any tears that might arise. If tears do fall, then let them come. That is what you have holes in your eyelids for... So let the tears come out. This releases pressure. Consider this the cleansing time before you take up any other primary meditations.

While practicing Forgiveness meditation, please use ONLY these meditation instructions and put all other meditation instructions aside until you have completed the work. This just means that we don't want to confuse mind, so, don't mix up the recipe! We want only the information needed to do this practice.

CHAPTER TWO – Instructions

The way you start practicing forgiveness meditation is by forgiving yourself.

There are different kinds of statements that you can use for this to help bring up any old grudges and hard-heartedness locked inside you. You may pick one statement to begin, and then you stay with that statement, for a period of time, to give it a chance to settle in and you and see what comes up. The first suggested phrase is **"I forgive myself for not understanding."** Everybody has misunderstandings that happen in their life. Nobody is exempt from this fact.

While you are sitting in meditation, you repeat the phrase, "I forgive myself for not understanding." After you've done that, you put that feeling and wish, into your heart and stay with that sense of forgiveness. When that feeling fades away, or the mind gets distracted, then you come back and forgive yourself for 'not understanding' yet again. Repeat the phrase to yourself.

This *is* a methodology. The way it works is below

Silently say the phrase to yourself: "I forgive myself for not understanding." Let it be an open statement or intention.

Continue with this phrase. As the feeling or the wish of Forgiveness fades then say the phrase again.

When a disturbing thought comes up about a past incident or person then *forgive that person – or yourself;* then <u>relax</u> any tightness that is left. There will be a painful feeling that arises and your mind won't like it! This where the Relax step is so important. If we react to the pain then this keeps the cycle going. You are feeding it through your aversion when you bring up this painful incident. You don't like and even hate this feeling. This leads to beating yourself up and not accepting that this is only a memory and it is long gone.

Accept whatever comes up and *forgive* and then *relax*.

Forgive, Relax This is what you do each time.

If it is just a distraction or a wandering mind then Forgive that too! Forgive anything that takes you away from forgiving yourself.

Then return to your phrase yet again "I forgive myself for not understanding…"

Do this cycle over and over. You forgive yourself first; you are the object of the meditation. Then while you are forgiving yourself you forgive anything that distracts you from wishing yourself forgiveness.

Gradually disturbances fade away and you are left with yourself – finally in the Present! Relief arises in the mind by throwing off these painful memories and letting go of the *reactive* mind that arises right after.

For those familiar with the Jhānas, and have meditated before, it is necessary to not go higher than the first jhāna. You can't mentally verbalize beyond that (say your phrases for forgiveness). Please make a determination to not go any deeper. This is an active contemplative process that we are doing now.

While you're doing this, your mind is going to have some resistance to this meditation. Your mind is going to take off and say, "Well, this is stupid - I shouldn't be doing this! Reactions like these are part of your attachments. These are the obstacles that we must dissolve.

Stay with your statement and repeat, "I forgive myself for not understanding." Then your mind might say, "AAH! I don't need to do this anymore. This meditation doesn't work". Every thought that pulls you away from forgiving yourself for not understanding is an attachment and has to be let go, and the tension and tightness in that attachment must be "relaxed" away.

This is where you will use your forgiveness. Any distractions or any sort of disturbances must be forgiven. To forgive we notice we have been distracted away from our object of meditation -or what we are doing in the present moment. We then *Forgive* the distraction and then *Relax*. Relax that tension and tightness that arises from the distraction or disturbance.

It doesn't matter how many times your mind gets distracted. One thing that many people get caught with is getting wrapped up in the story about things, and this can cause lots of pain and suffering and frustration. Forgiveness will help you with strong attachments and it shows the way to overcome the suffering that is caused. Recognize it. Let it be. Relax. Smile. Come back and stay with the wish of forgiveness for as long as you can.

Sitting should be followed by Walking Practice. If you are going to continue sitting again, or you are going to return to a task in daily life, before you do, take a stroll, at a normal pace to keep your blood flowing nicely. Walk for about 15 minutes minimum in some fresh air. 45 minutes is a good maximum time for walking. If you are working in a restricted space setting, find a space that is level and at least 30 feet long in length. Walk back and forth, and mentally, keep your meditation going.

*When you walk you want to walk in a way that you repeat the phrases with each stride as you walk. Like this: with the left foot take a step and mentally say **"I"** then a right step **"forgive"** and left **"you."** Then again, but say, **"You"** on the right step, and then left step, **"forgive,"** right step, **"me."** And repeat. Back and forth. You can experiment and see what works. It can get into a nice cadence but all the while it is really getting it into your 'noggin' to forgive! **"I forgive you, you forgive me."** And keep smiling when you are doing this. And *Forgive* anything or anyone who comes up that takes you away. Stay with the walking. I used to go for 6-8 mile walks in Hawaii doing just this practice!

The idea of sitting and walking is to create a continuous flow of meditation without stopping. This proves you can keep the meditation with you all the time in life. While walking at this normal pace, continue doing the forgiveness meditation with your eyes looking down towards the ground about 6 or 7 feet in front of you. Do not look around. Keep on gently forgiving. Keep smiling all the time.

CHAPTER THREE – Attachments

One mistake that an awful lot of people make is they say, "Well, meditation is just for sitting. The rest of the time I don't have anything else to do, so, I can let my mind act like it always does." This is a mistake. We need to consider the idea that Meditation is life and Life is meditation. You want to realize that you have attachments in your daily life and just because you are not sitting doesn't mean those attachments aren't there. The whole point in doing the meditation is for personality development. It's for letting go of old habitual suffering [bhava}, and in place of this, developing a mind that has equanimity in it.

The more resistance your mind has in doing this, the more you need to do it, because the resistance is your mind showing you where your attachment is, and that is the cause of suffering. This meditation works better than anything that I know of for letting go of attachments, letting go and relaxing of old hard-hearted feelings, letting go of the way you think the world is supposed to be, so you can start accepting the way the world actually is.

Your mind might say, "Well, I don't like that! I don't like the way they said this or that." Ask yourself now, "Who doesn't like it? Who is judging and condemning? Who is making up a story? Who is caught by their attachment?" "Well, 'I' am!"

It might be helpful here to give a definition of attachment. An attachment is anything we take personally, any thought, any feeling, any sensation! When we think these thoughts or feelings are "mine", this is "me", this is who "I" am, at that point, mind has become attached and this causes craving to arise in your mind and body.

Craving always manifests as a tension or tightness in both mind and body. Craving is the "I" like it, "I" don't like it mind - which arises in everyone's mind/body process. Attachment is another word for craving and is the start of all suffering. When we see that everything that arises is part of an impersonal process, then, we begin to understand what it is like to see things with a clear observant mind.

Somebody might say something very innocently and you hear it through your attachment and it's negative. This is why we have to learn how to become aware of what is happening all the time in our daily lives.

When you get finished sitting in your meditation for 30 minutes, 45 minutes, or for an hour and you start walking around, what does your mind do? It takes off just like it always does. It thinks about this. It thinks about that. These are just non-sense thoughts.

Most of us think those thoughts and those feelings that arise are ours personally; that they are not just random things. But, in truth, if you feed any kind of a thought or feeling with your attention, you make it bigger and more intense. When you realize that you are causing your own suffering, you have to forgive yourself for doing that.

This means saying, "I forgive myself for not understanding. I forgive myself completely." Of course, your mind is going to take off again and say,"Aah! This is stupid! This is nothing. This isn't real. This isn't what is actually happening. 'I' don't want to do this!"

Every one of those thoughts is an attachment, isn't it? Every one of those thoughts has craving in it, doesn't it? Every one of those thoughts is causing you suffering, right?

Because of this, you have to recognize that you are doing this to yourself and let go of those thoughts. That's just nonsense stuff anyway. It doesn't have anything to do with what you are doing and where you are right now. Once you know this, you forgive yourself for not understanding; for causing yourself pain; for causing other people pain. YOU REALLY FORGIVE.

Take a look at when you are walking from here to there. What are you doing with your mind? "Ho Hum. Thinking about this, and, I gotta do that, and, I have to go talk to that person, and, I have to do this." All of that's non-sense!

Now, this doesn't mean that you can't plan what you need to do next. You can. But just do that planning one time as your primary topic in the present moment. After you make up your mind what the plan is, you don't have to think about it anymore. Repeating it, rolling it around again; all of that is just part of your old habitual tendency (bhava in Pāli). It is your old, conditioned thoughts and feelings, and taking them personally and causing yourself pain and suffering.

CHAPTER FOUR – Daily Practice

Including the exercise of forgiveness in your daily activity is by far the most important part of this meditation. You forgive yourself continually, for not understanding, for getting caught up in this or that, for taking things personally. How many times have you found yourself doing this? "Hey! I don't like the way you said that." Ask yourself. WHO doesn't like what? "Well, you said something that was hurtful." To WHOM?

You need to stop and realize that you're taking all this stuff personally and it's not really personal. It's just stuff that happens. Forgive it! Forgive it even when you're walking along a road, and you happen to kick a rock, and it hurts. Forgive the pain for being there! Your job is to keep your mind forgiving all the time. That's what Mindfulness of Forgiveness Meditation practice is all about. The technique is not just about when you are sitting. This is a life practice. This is an all-the-time practice.

If you want to really begin to change, you have to be willing to go through the forgiveness sincerely, because it will help you change a lot. You have to have patience, and it helps to have a sense of humor about just how dumb mind can be. The more you smile and laugh the easier the meditation becomes.

CHAPTER FIVE - Finding Balance

Whenever you personally continue to think about this and that, to judge this and condemn that, you are constantly causing yourself suffering. You don't need to do that. You want to argue with other people about your attachments? What's the point? When you really start practicing forgiveness for yourself, or forgiveness for another person, your mind starts to get into balance, and your sense of humor begins to change. This is equanimity. Then you don't take thoughts, feelings and sensations and all this other stuff personally.

When you practice in this way, you are seeing life for what it is and allowing it to be there. It's not worth going over it in your mind, and over it, and over it, and over it. It's not worth it. It's a waste of time. It's a waste of effort. Every time you have a repeated thought, you are attached. You're identifying with that thought, and you're taking it personally, and that is again the cause of suffering. What you see here is the Second Noble Truth. You are witnessing how Craving, taking it personally is the cause of suffering. And you can't blame anybody else for it. It's yours. You are doing it all to yourself. "WELL, they said this!"

So what?

Others may have their opinion. That doesn't mean 'I' have to listen to them. I don't have to take it in personally and analyze whether it's correct or not because it doesn't matter. The more you forgive in your daily life and daily activities, the easier it is to forgive the big things that happened in the past.

CHAPTER SIX – Persistence

When you're doing the Forgiveness Meditation while you're sitting, you're staying with one of the suggested statements. You stay with that one statement until you internally feel, "YES, I really do forgive myself for not understanding." It's important to work this through.

To really forgive can take awhile. It's not just some quick fix to do in one sitting, and then you come in and say , "OK, now I'm done!", or you say, "I've already done that." Doing that is not where you're going to get real change. Nope. You still have your attachments there. You still have to continually forgive yourself for not understanding, forgive yourself for making a mistake. That is what not understanding is about. You have to forgive yourself for judging, for condemning, for analyzing, for thinking, for getting angry. Forgive everything, all of the time.

When I started to do the forgiveness meditation, which, I did personally for myself for two years, because I wanted to make sure I really understood this meditation, I went through major changes. There were major changes; major personality changes. If you want that for yourself, you have to have that kind of patience.

This idea of, "Well, I've already forgiven this person or that person," that simply isn't it. A little later on you figure out that you're talking about how YOU didn't like this or that from them! Ah! Guess what? Who hasn't finished their forgiveness meditation? YOU haven't forgiven yourself, or that other person!

CHAPTER SEVEN - Going Deeper

When you start to go deeper in your meditation, staying with the forgiveness, and you do forgive yourself for making mistakes, there can come a time when somebody comes up into your mind that you need to forgive.

When this happens, you realize that you did not ask them to come up. You do not stop and say, "Well, I need this person to come up." They came up by themselves.

As soon as that person comes up, you start forgiving them, for not understanding. It doesn't matter what they did in the past. All of your thoughts, all of your opinions of what they did in the past just keep bringing up more suffering.

These thoughts come up because of your attachment. "I didn't like that! I didn't want that to happen! They are a dirty no good so and so because they did that to me." Can you guess where the attachment is? Guess where the idea comes from that I can blame somebody else for my own suffering? The only person you can blame for your suffering is yourself. Why? Because YOU are the one that took it personally. You're the one who had an opinion about it. You're the one that used your habitual tendencies over and over again to justify the idea that I'm right and you're wrong. That's how we cause our own suffering.

The forgiveness meditation helps you let go of that opinion, that idea, that attachment, and feel some relief. Because some past person did or said something that caused anger, resentment, jealousy, pain or whatever the catch of the day was – it can have a real tendency for your mind to get caught up in thinking about that past event.

This is called getting caught by the story. You need to use the 6R's and then go back to your forgiveness statement. It doesn't matter how many times the story arises, please use the 6R's and then forgive again. The story's emotion will fade away after you do this enough. This is where patience is needed.

CHAPTER EIGHT - Letting Go

When you see someone else come up in your mind, somebody you really had a rough time with, and you didn't like it; someone you started hating for whatever reason, you forgive them. With your mind's eye, you look them straight in their eye, and you tell them sincerely: "I forgive you for not understanding the situation, I forgive you for causing me pain, I forgive you completely."

Now, keep that person in your heart and radiate forgiveness to them. If your mind has a distraction and it pulls you away from that; you might hear in your mind, "No, I don't, that no good so and so. I won't forgive him!" Using the 6R's, let go of this and come back and say, "I do forgive you."

It has to be sincere. "Well, I'm not going to forgive that dirty no good so and so." Why not? "Because they caused 'ME' suffering!" Oops! WHO caused who suffering? YOU caused your own self suffering because you took it personally, and YOU reinforced that with a lot of thoughts and opinions and ideas about why that was wrong.

In other words, you were caught in your craving, your own clinging, your habitual tendencies and that leads to more and more dissatisfaction, aversion, pain, and suffering.

CHAPTER NINE – Relief

It's really important to realize that this is not an easy practice. It's hard to forgive someone when they have really caused you harm. Take a woman that has been raped or a man who has been beaten and robbed. It's hard to forgive the person who raped them or beat them because they have been violated. But, holding onto their hatred of that person is keeping them attached. It doesn't matter what the action was. It doesn't matter what happened in the past. What matters is what you are doing with what you have in your mind right now.

To completely develop this practice to the highest level means that you keep forgiving and forgiving! Over and over. With your mind's eye, you look them straight in the eye, and you say, "I really do forgive you." And your mind says, "NO, I DON'T" And you let that go, and 6R, and come back. You say, "I really do forgive you." Then you take that person and put them into your heart and continue to radiate forgiveness to them. How long do you do that? As long as it takes.

For some attachments, one or two sittings are all you will need. Some other attachments might take a week; might take two weeks or even longer. Who knows? It doesn't matter. If you need time, you can take time! You have all the time there is.

You will feel a very, very strong sense of relief when you let go of the hatred you have towards these people. Then anytime you think of them, you kind of think of them with a mind that says, "Well, they made a mistake, they didn't know what they were doing. It's ok."

That's how you let go of an attachment (craving). That's how you let go of the pain of that past situation. This doesn't mean that the person who was violated is going to go up and hug the person who did that to them. They would avoid them because they know there is a possibility of personal harm. But they don't hate them anymore. They don't think about it anymore. They have let it go.

That's what the forgiveness is all about. It's about letting go. You are giving up old dissatisfaction and dislike. You are developing a mind that says, "Well that's ok. You can be like that." That is not taking it personally.

CHAPTER TEN – Obstacles

The biggest part of the Mindfulness of Forgiveness Meditation is learning how to let go of your personal opinions, ideas, concepts, stories. You might stay with a person for a long period of time because of your opinions and your attachment to this.

Every time you are doing any walking or sitting meditation, keep forgiving them over and over again. Your mind might get bored with that and say, "OH, I don't want to do this anymore!"

Well that's another kind of attachment, isn't it? So, what do you do with that? You have to get through it by forgiving the boredom for being there. That's ok. Your mind is tricky. It's going to try to distract you anyway it can. It'll bring up any kind of feelings and thoughts and ideas to distract you, because, it doesn't like the idea of giving up attachments. Your mind really feels comfortable, holding onto attachments.

We need to go easy on ourselves as we develop this practice. After all, how many years did it take us to build up our habits [bhava]? It takes patience to move in the opposite direction now and to change those unwholesome mind-states into new wholesome tendencies. Be kind to yourself and take your time.

The whole point of the Meditation is LEARNING HOW TO CHANGE. Learning how to let go of those old non-sense ideas and thoughts and develop new ideas and thoughts that make you happy and make other people around you happy too. That's the whole reason for the precepts. They outline an option for us to follow, so we gain balance in our life.

Let's take a quick look at the precepts. Do not kill any living beings on purpose. Don't take what is not freely given to you (no stealing). Don't engage in wrong sexual activity with another person's mate or a person too young living with their parents. In short, don't do anything that will cause mental or physical harm to any other human being. Don't engage in telling lies, using harsh language, gossip, or slander. Lastly, don't take recreational drugs or alcohol because these will weaken mind and the tendency to break the other precepts is stronger!

These precepts are like an ultimate operational manual for life. If you keep them well, then you get the most out of your life, they make you, and others around you happy. The more you can continually follow them, the better your frame of mind will become. You will more easily forgive that other person, your mind will become softer towards that person, and you will feel more relief.

What happens is, after you practice this way for a while, then you go "Ah, I do, I really do forgive you!" and there's no, energy behind it at all. It's just like, "yeah, this happened; it's in the past; it's no big deal." This is what forgiveness is all about.

CHAPTER ELEVEN – Daily Life

How can this practice affect your daily life? This is a good question. You're more open, you're more accepting. You're not judging. You're not condemning. You're not dis-liking, because as you see that tightness of mind coming up in you, and you go, "Oops! I forgive you for not understanding this one!", and your smile. You let it go.

One of the hardest things a guiding teacher has to do is to teach people that 'Life is supposed to be fun.' It's a game! Keep it light! If you, play with your mind and your attachments that means you are not being attached to them so much. As you play with them, you're not taking them so seriously anymore. When you don't take them seriously, they're easier to let go of.

That's what the Buddha was teaching us! He was teaching us how to have an uplifted mind all of the time; how to be able to be light with our thoughts, with our feelings, and our ideas, and our past actions.

Yes. It's true. On some occasions, you made a mistake. Well? Ok! Welcome to the human race! I don't know of anyone who hasn't made a mistake and felt guilty about it. Sure they do.

And what is that guilt? Non-forgiveness. That's an example of your mind grabbing onto what's happening and saying, "I really screwed up, and I need to punish myself for that." That's what your mind is saying. Now, do you see what you can do about this? Right! The more you become serious with your daily life, the more attachments you will have. The less equanimity, the less mental balance you will have in your life.

There is no question about it. You're on these roller coasters; emotional roller coasters, up and down, up and down, up and down. When you start forgiving more, those high highs, and low lows start to turn into little waves. You still have some. But you don't get caught for as long. You just stop and say, "This just isn't important enough to get upset about."

CHAPTER TWELVE – Success!

After you forgive that person, you stay with them; you stay with that person that's come up into your mind until you feel like, "Enough! I don't have to do this anymore. I really have forgiven you." At that point, with your mind's eye, you look them straight in the eye, and you stop verbalizing, and you hear them say back to you: "I forgive you too."

Wow! Now this is different, isn't it? It's kind of remarkable. You have this feeling of being forgiven as well as you forgiving them! You've forgiven yourself for making mistakes, for not understanding. You've forgiven that other person for making mistakes, for not understanding, or causing pain, whatever you want using the statement that really makes it true for you. And, now, you hear them say "I forgive you."

There is a real sense of relief. Wow! What happens in your mind now is that JOY comes up in your mind. You feel light. You feel really happy. Happier than you ever felt before. You didn't realize you were carrying these big bundles of rocks on your shoulders, holding you down, did you? And now, you have put them down. When you forgive, the heaviness of those hard feelings and "rocks" disappear. You feel light. "Oh My! This REALLY is great stuff!"

It takes a lot of work, but, it's worth it. It's not easy. Why isn't it easy? Because of the amount of attachment we have when we begin. You keep doing the meditation, and when you get done with one person, you go back to yourself. You repeat: "I forgive myself for making mistakes. I forgive myself for not understanding." You stay with yourself until somebody else comes up into your mind. You keep on doing that until your mind says, "OK. I've done it. Everything is good. There's nobody else. Enough!"

At this time, you can switch back to your Mindfulness of Loving-Kindness meditation and make it your primary formal practice. Now you can understand why Mindfulness of Forgiveness Meditation is definitely part of Loving-Kindness. How can you ever practice Loving-Kindness if you have hatred? You can't. This practice releases the Hatred.

CHAPTER THIRTEEN – Not Easy

This practice has NO simple, easy, fast-fix here! You can't just buy the solution this time at the Mall either. You have to patiently continue this practice all the time until you release the unwholesome mind-states which are your old habitual tendencies of mind.

Depending on how attached you are to the idea that a person wronged you, or the idea of how badly you screwed up, this leads you into "I can never forgive myself." Until you finally go through this process of forgiveness, you will not be free of this burden.

You WILL know when you have gone entirely through the Mindfulness of Forgiveness Meditation because then you will be free and you will see clearly this is how Forgiveness really works. Are you done? You don't have to have anybody to tell you that this worked. You'll know!

The daily continuous work of this practice is most important. When you are walking from one place to another, I don't care what you are doing. Any kind of distraction that comes up forgive it. Smile. If a person comes up to you and they start talking, and you don't want to talk, FORGIVE THEM. They don't understand. They don't understand what you are doing. It's ok that they don't understand. It's ok that they don't know where you are or what you are doing. They can judge you, they can condemn you, they can cause all kinds of distractions, and that's fine. They can do that. BUT, as for you, you can forgive them for it.

As you forgive them, you are letting go of the attachment to the way 'I' think things are supposed to be. Not understanding can be a really big thing. Because we don't understand so much; we have our own opinions and ideas of the way things are supposed to work; that can be a problem. We get caught up by assumption. That's it, isn't it?

What happens when things don't match your idea of the way things are supposed to work? What then? You may find yourself fighting with REALITY which is the truth, the Dhamma of the present moment! You're not accepting the reality that's right there in front of you. You begin judging and condemning, and, most often, blaming somebody else for, disturbing you.

Well, I'm sorry... They're not disturbing your practice. THEY ARE PART OF THE PRACTICE! There's no such thing as something else, or someone else, disturbing MY PRACTICE. It's only me fighting with what is real, the REALITY, the Dhamma of the present moment, not liking this or that, and next, I am blaming somebody else OR something else for the cause of that...

CHAPTER FOURTEEN – Forgive it!

What about sounds disturbing us while we practice? Sometimes, in a retreat, if you are concentrating too hard you can observe what can happen. You could get SO upset if there is even one squeak of a door or someone is walking by too heavily near you or breathing too loudly. You might jump up thinking "OH! You disturbed my practice!"

Do you begin to see how ridiculous this actually is? What is happening here is that the present moment produced a noise, and there was noise, and then, mind came up and said, "I don't like this. That's not supposed to be there." "I want to complain to somebody, and make them stop so MY mind can be peaceful!" What is actually happening is concentration is out of balance with mindfulness. Concentration is too strong, and mindfulness is too weak. Hahaha! How crazy is that?

If you can't accept what's happening in the present moment, with a balanced mind, there will be suffering. OK! So! There's a noise. "Somebody is talking!" So? It doesn't matter just as long as you have mindfulness and equanimity in your mind. When balance is in your mind, if there is a noise, that's just fine. And? You can do your forgiveness meditation!

While I was in Asia on a three-month retreat. There was a water well pump that was drilling for water right outside of the meditation hall. Three months of an old clanky motor running from 8 a.m. until 6 p.m. This can happen, you know? One continuous noise! It was really loud and really annoying, but, it was just sound. That's all it was. I realized that it was not "My" sound. "'My" dislike of that sound wasn't going to change that sound. "My" criticizing of the person that started the motor wasn't going to make that sound any different.

Do you see where all the attachments are in this example? The exercise here is accepting the fact that sound is here, and it's ok for sound to be here. It has to be ok, because, that's what's in the present moment. That's the truth [Dhamma]. Accepting the present moment is accepting the Dhamma just as it is.

Whenever there is a disturbance, forgive the disturbance continually in your mind. FORGIVE. Smile. Forgive yourself for not understanding. That is how we work with forgiveness in daily life. I forgive myself for wanting things to be more perfect than they are. I forgive myself for making mistakes. I forgive myself for being angry, and, disliking this or that. Now we see that the forgiveness is not just one statement, it can be many. We take each of these statements into the practice and use them one by one.

CHAPTER FIFTEEN – No Mantras

While you're doing your sitting practice, once again, you just want to take one statement of forgiveness at a time. Stay with just one. Remember that this is not a mantra. You don't surface say this and think about something else either. It has to be sincere. "I really do forgive myself for making mistakes or for not understanding or whatever." It's important to be sincere when you do this.

The more you can continually forgive, with your daily activities, with your sitting, with your walking meditation, whatever you happen to be doing; you need to realize that this is what meditation is really about.

Meditation is not about gaining some super-human state of mind. It's not just about bliss. It is more productive than that. It's about learning how you cause your own suffering and how to let go of that suffering. The deeper super-human states of meditation will come up by themselves when we clear our minds and simply allow this to happen. You don't have to personally do anything.

The more you clear yourself, the more you clear your mind of judgments, opinions, concepts, ideas, and the more you accept what's happening in the present moment, the more joyful life becomes. The easier life becomes.

What's that you are saying now? "Well, I have this habit of always analyzing and thinking." OK, let it go. "BUT I have been doing this my whole life." So? Hey! Forgive yourself for not understanding. Forgive yourself for analyzing.

There can be a strong attachment to wanting to analyze. That's the Western disease. "I want to know how everything works." You don't learn how things work by thinking about them. You let go and relax to see how things work when you forgive, and, you let go and relax to develop space in your mind to observe how they work.

The truth is that, in meditation, thinking mind, analyzing mind is incredibly slow. The aware mind is incredibly fast. It's extraordinary! You just can't get there with a lot of words in the way. You can't have opinions in the way. They will block you. They will stop you from seeing the way things truly are.

CHAPTER SIXTEEN – Blame Game

Your Forgiveness Meditation is more than just about old attachments like, "Well, when I was five years old, Little Johnny, he beat me up, and I've hated him ever since then." See how this is about you and uncovering this attachment and how you hold onto it, and how you cause yourself pain because of that attachment?

Most especially these days, people are really big on blaming everybody but themselves for their pain, and, the question here should be, is that working with reality or not? It's easy to say, "YOU caused me pain. I don't like you." But, did someone else cause you pain? Or did I just say something and you had another kind of an opinion, and, judged and condemned whatever I said, and then, your aversion came up, and the dislike of the whole situation, and now, you're off to the races, and you're a thousand miles away.

You are causing yourself pain, and you're running into your thinking, "But, I'm only thinking and analyzing." Ha ha ha ha ha! You're attached! You think, "This attachment won't hurt me so much if I keep distracted. I can keep MY opinions, and my ideas about the way things are supposed to be, and then, I don't have to change!" But, you're fooling yourself. Change is the only way to free mind. Meditation is about positive change.

CHAPTER SEVENTEEN – Be Happy!

In summary, BUDDHISM is about realizing that you need to have a balanced and mindful mind, that doesn't have high emotions in it, that doesn't' have attachments in it so that you can see things clearly and discover real happiness and contentment in daily life.

BUDDHISM is about seeing the way things truly are; gaining knowledge by seeing for yourself how you are the cause of your own pain. It's about taking personal responsibility and doing the work needed to find this kind of mindfulness, balance, and understanding.

Mindfulness of Forgiveness Meditation trains us to recognize clearly when suffering arises [First Noble Truth], to notice how we get personally involved with it and make it bigger which causes more suffering in life [Second Noble Truth], and to escape this dangerous trap by using the 6R's and seeing how it disappears [Third Noble Truth]; This meditation opens the way for clear understanding and relief [Fourth Noble Truth].

The end-result creates the space we need in our mind so that we begin to respond to life instead of reacting. Using the 6R's, which fulfills the practice of Right Effort found in the early texts; using it with any meditation you are doing, is one of the fastest ways for all people to see clearly what is really going on and to reach this kind of destination where there can be happiness and Peace.

In sutta number 21 of the Majjhima Nikāya, as translated by Bhikkhu Bodhi, within The Middle Length Sayings' and published by Wisdom Publications, it gives us some excellent advice that I would like to share with you now. It says:

"There are these five courses of speech that others may use when they address you, their speech may be timely or untimely, true or untrue, gentle or harsh, connected with good or connected with harm, spoken with a mind of loving-kindness or with inner hatred.

"This is how I should train: My mind shall be unaffected, and I will utter no evil words; I shall abide compassionate for their welfare, with a mind of loving-kindness, without inner hate. I shall abide pervading that person (whoever you talk with) with a mind imbued with loving-kindness (and forgiveness) and starting with him, I shall abide pervading the all-encompassing world with a mind imbued with loving-kindness, abundant, exalted, immeasurable, without hostility and ill-will". That is how I should train.

Please use this Forgiveness Meditation often and train your mind to be happy

Printed in Great Britain
by Amazon